Mufacing THE USIC

facing THE MUSIC

Faith and Meaning in Popular Songs

Darrell W. Cluck
Catherine S. George
J. Clinton McCann, Jr.

Chalice Press
St. Louis, Missouri

Cover: Kevin Darst
Interior design: Elizabeth Wright

This book is printed on acid-free, recycled paper.

Visit Chalice Press on the World Wide Web at
www.chalicepress.com

10 9 8 7 6 5 4 3 2 1   99 00 01 02 03

Library of Congress Cataloging–in–Publication Data

Cluck, Darrell W.
  Facing the music : faith and meaning in popular songs / by Darrell W. Cluck, Catherine S. George, J. Clinton McCann, Jr.
      p.   cm.
  Includes bibliographical references.
  ISBN 0-8272-1022-1
  1. Music in Christian education. 2. Popular music--Religious aspects--Christianity. 3. Christian education of young people.   I. George, Catherine S. II. McCann, J. Clinton, 1951-   .   III. Title.
BV1534.8.C57   1999   98–41531
261.5'78--dc21   CIP

Printed in the United States of America

The authors lovingly dedicate this book
to their children,

Robbie Cluck

Sam George

Shelley George

Meredith George

Jennifer McCann

Sarah McCann

with deep gratitude to them
for helping us face the music.

Contents

Authors' Acknowledgments

I wondered what acknowledge meant
When it appears within a book.
So, over my keyboard I bent
And, thus, this chancy route I took:
To thank the God to whom I'm bound,
Both now, and for eternity.
To thank Montreat, for there I found
The music in my ministry.
To thank my church, for graciously
They share the Pastor whom they pay.
To thank my wife who patiently
Still tolerates my teenage way.
To thank my colleagues last, not less;
For Clint and Cathy, both, have been
Embodiments of helpfulness.
And now the sequel we begin.

Darrell Cluck

I am continually awed and amazed, not to mention humbled, by the many ways God blesses me through the faithful care of some incredible people. They are truly incarnations of God's grace: my parents, Joan and John Sharp, and my whole family for always being ready with a warm welcome when I round the bend to the farm; my funny, fun, and loving "Dallas event in wherever it is/Alabama gang"–

Patti Winter, Randy Jackson, Phyllis Ward, and Monty Clendenin; the other two "scary women," Beth Elliott and Vicki Collins, who love me, challenge me, and stand by me with amazing strength and help me find clarity when the way gets foggy; Sharon Yunker-Deatz; Judy and Charlie Chandler; and my children, Sam, Shelley, and Meredith, who "allow" me the gift of being their mom and their friend. The reality of actually writing an acknowledgment piece for this book reminds me of my gratitude to Clint, for giving words to the dream, and to Darrell for dreaming the dream and then graciously inviting me in.

Cathy George

A jointly authored book is obviously a communal endeavor, but the contributions to this effort extend far beyond those of Darrell, Cathy, and me. First of all, however, my thanks go to the following:

Darrell and Cathy for their ideas, their energy, their enthusiasm, their friendship, and their commitment to the church and its ministry, especially ministry with and for young people.

Thanks also to my daughters, Jennifer and Sarah, who urged me to attend the Rock Seminar (led by Darrell and Cathy) at the 1995 Montreat Conference on Music and Worship, an event that laid the foundation for future cooperation among Darrell, Cathy, and me.

They are too many to name individually, but thanks too to my colleagues and students at Eden Theological Seminary, especially those who introduced me to new songs and loaned me tapes and CDs. Special thanks to those who read and commented upon portions of the manuscript: Sarah Fredriksen, Jeff Groene, Doug Kaufman, Karl Kuhn, Susan Niesen, and Ed Zumwinkel. And, as always, many thanks to Mary Swehla, Administrative Assistant to the Faculty, who word-processed much of the manuscript and without whom I could do virtually nothing.

Thanks also to the artists who create poetry and music that is capable of reaching people in ways that not only entertain but also inspire and teach. Several artists have taken a special interest in this volume. They and/or their representatives have encouraged us and contributed ideas and material over and above their music, and we thank them: Tori Amos, Bruce Cockburn, David LaMotte, and Noel Paul Stookey. Thanks also to the artists and their representatives who gave us permission to quote from their songs without fee: Tori Amos, Bruce Cockburn, David LaMotte, Natalie Merchant, Metallica, and Noel Paul Stookey.

And thanks finally to the staff of Chalice Press and Christian Board of Publication, especially to academic editor Jon Berquist, who showed an initial interest in this project and who has provided helpful advice along the way; to editor-in-chief David Polk, who also responded favorably to this project and whose editorial expertise has guided it to completion; to marketing manager Susie Burgess, who has provided us helpful information and materials; and to Russ White, President of Christian Board of Publication, whose friendship and support has been an encouragement.

Clint McCann

Introduction

Why Popular Songs?

The Christian faith is essentially incarnational: "The Word *became flesh* and lived among us" (Jn. 1:14). This summary of the good news has proven, of course, to be persistently problematic. It means that God has chosen to reveal God's own self in *human* terms—in human culture, in human structures, even in human flesh ("incarnate" means "to enflesh").

It may seem problematic enough to affirm that a human being, Jesus of Nazareth, incarnates God; but the Gospel of John is just getting started at this point! By the end of the Gospel, John affirms that after the human Jesus has left the world, the Spirit represents his ongoing presence (Jn. 14:15–17). And what's more, the Spirit is revealed *in the church*—a *human* structure (Jn. 20:19–23). Obviously, the possibility for ambiguity is paramount![1] It is easy to identify countless historical and contemporary instances in which the church has not and does not act very Christlike. As 2 Corinthians 4:7 puts it, we represent Christ as "clay jars" (NRSV) or "earthen vessels" (RSV), but such ambiguity is the unavoidable price of an incarnational faith.

In its wisdom, however, the church has decided that the advantages of an incarnational faith far outweigh the disadvantages. On the supremely positive side, the good news of

1

the Incarnation is that God honors humankind enough to be one of us—in John's terms, "God so loved the world" (3:16).[2] Or, in the words of one of the characters in Andre Dubus's short story, "A Father's Story": "Belief is believing in God; faith is believing that God believes in you."[3] The Incarnation affirms that God believes in us! One of the practical effects of God's belief in us is that God is revealed in human institutions, human structures, human cultures. It is the thesis of this book that God can be revealed in and through popular songs, and we intend to demonstrate how this may indeed actually happen.

Admittedly, to some people, this may sound strange, or even impossible. Some Christians have opposed popular music—especially rock and roll—as dangerous, even demonic. Other Christians have opposed popular music as simply too common, too culturally and artistically inferior, to have any positive use for religious purposes. But that God may be revealed in popular music—that is, the music *of the people*—is really not so strange or unlikely.

People, or at least God's people, have always used their own artistic creations for the purpose of worshiping God and instructing others about God. Some of these poems and songs are, of course, in the Bible: the Song of Miriam (Ex. 15:20–21), the Song of Moses (Deut. 32:1–43), the Song of Deborah and Barak (Judg. 5:1–31), the Book of Psalms. The early Christian community continued the practice of singing "psalms" and "hymns," which it found in the Old Testament, but it apparently also introduced nonbiblical "spiritual songs" (Col. 3:16). In any case, at some point, there arose the practice that most Christians take for granted today—the collection of nonbiblical poems set to music in books usually called "hymnals."

But, some will still object, these hymnals at least contain "spiritual songs" or "church music"—that is, material that has been tested by years of use so as to have become part of a liturgical tradition. This is true, of course; but "church music," or the "liturgical tradition," has not ever been and is not a monolithic, static entity. It has changed, is changing, and will always change. In the Reformation era, for instance,

John Calvin, Martin Luther, and others effected a monumental change in the church's liturgical tradition. In the early sixteenth century, singing was the domain of highly trained and musically sophisticated monastic choirs. The Reformers wanted to make singing an activity in which the whole church participated. As Martin Luther is supposed to have framed the issue, "Why let the devil have all the good tunes?"[4] In other words, the music that the people knew and could actually sing consisted of barroom ditties and folk tunes. What did the Reformers do? They adopted these tunes for use in the church, and they adapted the songs by supplying scriptural words (often from the Book of Psalms) or spiritual poetry for the familiar tunes.

To be sure, there was opposition and objection to the Reformers' innovations. Interestingly, the reasons given then are similar to reasons given now to ignore popular music; for instance, it carries negative associations, and it is culturally unsophisticated and artistically inferior. Registering her objection to the Reformation's new practice of metrical psalmody, Queen Elizabeth I called the songs "Geneva jigs."[5] What is revealing, however, is that the Reformers were intent on meeting people where they were; and thus they were not deterred from using even the "devil's tunes" in church!

It is precisely this Reformation principle—meeting people where they are and using their music—that provides a primary motivation for this book. We assume that people who listen to the kind of music we are calling "popular"—primarily rock and roll of several varieties (alternative, hard, soft, etc.), but also some folk, rhythm and blues, and even a bit of disco and country—are persons who are approximately age fifty-four and under. That is to say, they are primarily the Baby Boomers (born 1943–1960) and the members of a generation variously known as "Generation X," the "Thirteenth Generation," or the Baby Busters (born 1961–1981), but also the older members of the most recent generation, the "Millennial Generation" (born after 1982).[6] One of the interesting things about music is its ability to unite people. For instance, Clint has discovered that he (born 1951), his older daughter (Jennifer, born 1981), and his younger daughter

(Sarah, born 1986) generally like to listen to the same popular songs! The same is true for Darrell (born 1950) and his son Robbie (born 1981), as well as for Cathy (born 1953) and her children, Sam (born 1974), Shelley (born 1977), and Meredith (born 1980). In other words, on some level at least, the generation gap is being bridged by way of mutual listening to Alanis Morissette, Natalie Merchant, Joan Osborne, Billy Joel, the Dave Matthews Band, Dishwalla, and a host of others.

This discovery in itself may be interesting, but it becomes something more than merely interesting in view of the fact that the church has largely failed to retain or attract Generation X. Consequently, as Jay Hudson has put it, "the most crucial issue facing the church in [North] America in the next ten years is whether or not we will choose to minister with Generation X."[7] It is clear that some congregations have chosen to try to minister with and to Generation X. These congregations have sought innovative ways to proceed, including going beyond traditional "church music," especially in services variously known as contemporary services, outreach services, seeker services, user-friendly worship, etc. This direction is crucial. Not only may it have the potential to reach several generations simultaneously, but it is probably absolutely essential to reaching Generation X (and perhaps the Millennial Generation, about which it is still too early to generalize). As Hudson says:

> Music is the soul of this generation. No one style of music speaks to the entire age group, but refusing to acknowledge the alternative music genre in the church is to say "no" to a generation.[8]

To be sure, what it means "to acknowledge the alternative music genre in the church" is not entirely clear; it will almost certainly mean a variety of things. For some pastors, worship committees, and church musicians, it may mean exploring the actual use of popular songs, or at least new genres of music, in worship.[9] For other pastors, it may mean using popular songs in constructive ways to illustrate biblical and theological affirmations in sermons. For religious educators, it may mean constructing curricula using popular songs as points of departure. For church school teachers, youth ministers, and youth advisors, it may mean using popular songs in lessons, programs, and retreats. For parents and children, it may be a way of initiating conversations with each other.

It is the purpose of this book to serve as a resource for pursuing all of the above possibilities for exploring what it means "to acknowledge the alternative music genre in the church." In other words, we want to help the church in "facing the music" that pervades our culture and that indeed may be the very soul of the younger generation(s). The music is there, and it will be there, whether we like it or not. To be sure, the church can turn the other way, but not without great loss. By facing the music, we choose to take people seriously and to meet them where they are. Not only is this good pastoral care, but as suggested earlier, it is also a contemporary application of the Reformation principle of using the music *of the people* to facilitate their participation in worship and their growth in faith. Thus, by facing the music, we are being faithful to the Reformation tradition, and indeed ensuring that the Reformation tradition still represents reform. Furthermore, we are being faithful to the Bible itself. For ultimately, we are compelled to face the music, because we believe that God reveals God's own self in human flesh, including human cultural productions like popular songs. In our view, by facing the music, we stand to learn about about the nature of God (chapter 1), about ourselves as human beings (chapter 2), about Jesus Christ (chapter 3), about the church (chapter 4), and about the church's God-given mission in the world (chapter 5). As the conclusion will suggest, the ultimate purpose of this book is, as is every proclamation of the Gospel, to invite transformation–to change people, to change the church, to change the world.

Popular Songs as Witness

The reader will inevitably raise the following question: What led us to choose the particular songs that will be featured in this book? One criterion for our choices, of course, is that the songs were actually "popular", that is to say, they were widely listened to and liked by many people. In other words, the songs somehow made an impact on people and even on our society. One perhaps could say that the songs "worked," or that their musical excellence was recognized. Marva Dawn describes excellent music as follows:

> Music of excellence makes use of interesting melodies and/or rhythms and accompaniments appropriate to the subject, melody, and rhythm. It is not bland, plodding, inert, or trite. A good test for excellence is whether we can stand to listen to the music (without the words) over and over several times without getting tired of it.[10]

Needless to say, young people are notorious (especially in their parents' opinion) for listening to the same songs over and over again. They thereby reveal what they consider to be "excellent." The songs featured in the following chapters are ones that we ourselves, along with millions of other people, have listened to "over and over...without getting tired of" them.

To be sure, however, popularity alone does not make a song suitable for a book like this. Lots of people, for instance, may like songs that are vulgar, violent, or vacuous. We have paid particular attention to the *content* of popular songs; and we have chosen ones that, with appropriate commentary at least, may serve as witnesses to the Gospel of Jesus Christ and to the commitments to which the Gospel calls us. This is not to say that the writers and performers of these songs intended their work to be Christian or even religious. In some cases, they clearly did have this intention; but in most cases, they did not. Even so, their work can be sources for what Paula J. Carlson and Peter S. Hawkins call "listening for God." Although Carlson and Hawkins are speaking about "listening for God" in contemporary literature, what they say also applies to popular songs:

> Listening for God...means allowing yourself to listen to the sounds of your own culture in all its

bewildering diversity but without knowing for sure what you'll find. [11]

What Carlson and Hawkins call "allowing yourself to listen to the sounds of your own culture" is what we are calling "facing the music." In essence, what we have done first of all is to face the music, to listen to the sounds of our culture in the form of popular songs, and in so doing, we have found ourselves hearing a witness to God.

To be sure, as a pastor, a seminary student, and a seminary professor, we are accustomed to "listening for God." Our vocation and our training certainly lead us to hear things in popular songs that others may not hear and that the writers or performers may not have intended. In short, our main purpose is to share what we have heard in "listening for God" as we have listened to popular songs. What this will mean is that each song will be related both to the Bible and to the church's theological tradition. Thus, popular songs serve as a witness to God insofar as they are heard in conversation with the Bible and its theological claims. In sharing the witness to God that we have heard in popular songs, we hope also to inspire you to continue to allow "yourself to listen to the sounds of your own culture" as a way of "listening for God"–and we hope, too, to instruct you on what to listen for as you face the music.

This latter hope or intention addresses the major problem of a book like this one–namely, that it may appear to be outdated by the time it is published, since new "popular songs" are appearing all the time. One response to this objection is to point out that many of the songs we discuss in the following chapters are "classics." They will remain "popular" for years to come, and many of them will continue to be heard regularly on the radio, especially on stations whose format is something like "the best of the eighties and the nineties." But beyond this fact, it should be noted that we are attempting to model a method or an approach. We hope that by sharing what we have heard, we will teach others what to listen for in new songs.

Using This Book: Suggestions and an Example

How one uses this book will depend on one's interests and purposes. As suggested earlier, it can be used to get in touch with material for use in sermon illustration, in curriculum development, in youth and retreat programming, and possibly even in liturgical settings. In any case, the first step in pursuing any of these purposes is to listen to the music itself. Often the words to a song will be printed on the booklet that accompanies the compact disc or cassette, and the words can frequently be found on the internet. The material included in each chapter of this book is intended to facilitate biblical and theological reflection on the songs. For pastors, educators, and youth leaders who want to use the songs in programming (Bible study, discussion groups, retreats, church school, etc.), see the appendices at the end of this volume. They provide further information on the songs and artists, helpful advice for using the songs in programming, and suggested questions for discussion.

In some instances, the popular songs included in the following chapters are available on both compact disc/cassette tape and as a video. In many instances, though not all, the video greatly enhances the interpretive directions and possibilities of a song. Consider, for instance, Madonna's "Like A Prayer." To be sure, the initial issue to be faced in considering the use of this song/video may be Madonna's controversial reputation. Those who decide to use it may want to explain that the use of the song/video does not constitute blanket approval of Madonna's values and lifestyle. In any case, if this issue can be successfully negotiated, the song/video becomes available as a resource that offers a trenchant criticism of racism and injustice, and indeed, one that is based on explicitly christological grounds!

In the video, one of the main characters, a white woman (played by Madonna) witnesses the attack of another woman by a band of white men, whom she apparently knows. She also sees that after the perpetrators flee, a black man arrives on the scene, tries to help the victim, and is arrested for the crime when the police arrive. Wrestling with her dilemma, the woman goes to an African American church. There she sees a statue of a black Jesus. In a dream sequence, she sees the black Jesus shed a tear and speak to her "like a prayer." In the dream, the Jesus figure comes to life and leaves the church shortly before the woman reviews the sequence of events involved in the crime. This sequence leads the woman to a recognition that she articulates in response to Jesus: "You are not what you seem." In other words, in a moment of revelation, the woman realizes that Jesus is revealed by the black man arrested for the crime and now in jail. Having seen Jesus in the least of one of her brothers (see Matt. 25:40, 45), she visits the jail and offers her eyewitness testimony, which leads to the accused man's release. This act illustrates, in essence, the risk of discipleship, recalling that earlier in the video, the woman had envisioned the wounds of Jesus as stigmata on her own hands.[12]

Not only does one hear resonances of Matthew 25:31–46 in the video, but also the woman's experience of Jesus recalls Luke 7:36–50, the story of the disreputable woman who anoints and kisses Jesus' feet. At one point in the video, the woman kisses the feet of the black Jesus. To be sure, this introduces an element of sensuality that some may find uncomfortable or even obscene. But the sensuality of the video is hardly, if at all, equal to that of Luke 7:36–50.[13] The effect of the video is to emphasize Jesus' humanity, something the church has rarely taken very seriously. The further effect, of course, is to suggest that the real obscenity in our society is the racism that has and does regularly victimize African Americans.

Perhaps because of the sensuality of the video, or perhaps because it depicts burning crosses in the background at one point, the Roman Catholic Church banned "Like A Prayer." But, as suggested earlier, the sensuality of the video is not unbiblical, and the burning crosses are intended not to be sacriligious, but rather to represent the racism fostered by white supremicists like members of the Ku Klux Klan, who take God's name in vain by burning crosses to intimidate those whom they hate. The video is finally both a denunciation of racism on christological grounds, as well as an anticipation of the new community that Jesus gathered and still gathers around him. As a result of hearing the black Jesus "call my name," the white woman in the video finds a welcoming community among the members of the African American church. This newfound community contrasts sharply with the woman's initial conclusion that "everyone must stand alone." The remarkable transformation is marked ultimately by the woman's response to having been called by name: "It feels like home." In a society saturated with discrimination, racism, and violence, the church should welcome any work of art, especially one that many people will hear and see, that offers a compelling vision of inclusivity, community, and love.

Then too, one might observe that "Like A Prayer" pushes toward a deeper understanding of prayer. People usually think of prayer as talking to God, whereas the video suggests that prayer also essentially involves listening for God, an activity that is at the heart of what we mean by facing the music.

NOTES

[1] For a penetrating analysis of John's christology, see Robin Scroggs, *Christology in Paul and John* (Philadelphia: Fortress, 1988), pp. 55–102, esp. 78–91.

[2] See chapter 2 for a consideration of a song titled "One of Us," by Joan Osborne.

[3] Andre Dubus, *Selected Stories* (New York: Vintage Books, 1988), p. 461.

[4] Cited in Marva J. Dawn, *Reaching Out Without Dumbing Down: A Theology of Worship for Turn-of-the-Century Church* (Grand Rapids: Eerdmans, 1995), p. 189.

[5] For a brief account of the rise of metrical psalmody in the Reformation era, see Hughes Oliphant Old, *Worship that Is Reformed According to Scripture*, Guides to the Reformed Tradition (Atlanta: John Knox, 1984), pp.47-55.

[6] For this generational analysis, see William Strauss and Neil Howe, *Generations: The History of America's Future, 1584 to 2069* (New York: William Morrow, 1991), as cited in Jay Hudson, "The Thirteenth Generation: Demographics and Worship," *Reformed Liturgy and Music* 30/2 (1996): 43-47.

[7] "The Thirteenth Generation," p. 43.

[8] Ibid., p. 47.

[9] For helpful criteria for assessing the suitability of music for use in worship, see Marva J. Dawn, *Reaching Out Without Dumbing Down*,165-204. See also Tim and Kathy Carson, *So You're Thinking About Contemporary Worship* (St. Louis: Chalice Press, 1997), especially pp. 67-76.

[10] *Reaching Out Without Dumbing Down*, p.198.

[11] Paula J. Carlson and Peter S. Hawkins, eds., *Listening for God: Contemporary Literature and the Life of Faith* (Minneapolis: Augsburg Fortress, 1994), p. 7.

[12] For a different interpretation of the video, see Tom Beaudoin, *Virtual Faith: The Irreverent Spiritual Quest of Generation X* (San Francisco: Jossey-Bass, 1998), pp. 74-75. Beaudoin suggests that the statue represents not Jesus, but rather Saint Martin de Porres (1579–1639), whose father was Spanish and whose mother was black. St. Martin worked in Peru among the ill, the poor, and the enslaved, and the Roman Catholic tradition views him "as the patron saint of interracial justice" (p. 75). Beaudoin concludes that "Madonna's relationship with this important saint represents a strong critique of American race relations" (p. 75). We fully agree with this conclusion, although we have reached this conclusion by way of a different understanding of the video.

[13] For an exposition of the shocking sensuality of Lk. 7:36-50, see Marcus J. Borg, *Jesus, a New Vision: Spirit, Culture, and the Life of Discipleship* (San Francisco: Harper, 1987), pp. 134, 146.

ONE

Facing the Music about God

Thinking about God

Thinking about God as a Witness to the Gospel

The subtitle to this chapter alludes to the subtitle of Dishwalla's song titled "Counting Blue Cars": "Tell Me All Your Thoughts on God." It is a rather explicit invitation to think about God, and thinking about God is certainly an essential component of what the Introduction called "listening for God." In fact, "thinking about God" could serve as a definition of the term *theology*! Despite this fact, of course, many Christians have been taught not to think about God. Rather they have been advised that Christianity is a matter of accepting things "on faith" without trying to understand.

While there is undoubtedly an essential and ultimately inexplicable mystery that lies at the heart of the Christian faith (see below), the advice not to think about God is dangerously misleading and ultimately destructive of genuine faith for the following reasons.

First of all, the history of humankind, ancient or modern, reveals that human beings simply cannot *not* think about God. Dishwalla's "Counting Blue Cars" features a child who, quite typically, has lots of questions. But the fact of the matter, of course, is that it is not just children who have questions. Human beings of all ages in all places and times have had and still have many fundamental questions about their origin, their existence, and the ultimate meaning of their lives—in short, questions about God. To advise people not to confront these questions—in essence, not to think about God—is unrealistic, uncaring, and unfaithful. Indeed, it is likely that many persons in recent years have been driven away from the church by the advice of pastors and other church leaders not to think about God. We live in a society that highly values education and critical thinking in every field and endeavor except religion. It's as if the church has asked people to turn off their minds as they enter the sanctuary. Therefore, it is no wonder that at least one of the primary reasons for the decline of the so-called "mainline" denominations is the church's failure to encourage persons to seek an intellectually honest and satisfying understanding of God and the Christian faith. Or, to use Dishwalla's subtitle, we have alienated people insofar as we have refused to honor their questions and insofar as we have been unwilling to say, simply and directly to people, "Tell Me All Your Thoughts on God."

Secondly, the advice not to think about God represents a dangerous misunderstanding of what faith is essentially all about. In biblical terms, faith is not primarily intellectual assent to a series of propositions or doctrines. Rather, faith is the entrusting of one's whole life to God, including the life of the mind. Important consequences follow from the biblical understanding of faith as essentially trust rather than belief. For instance, we are set free to pursue the Augustinian direction of faith seeking understanding. That is, we are set free to think critically and creatively about God and God's character without having to worry that we are insulting God by way of our questions and without ever having to claim that we have finally arrived at figuring God out. Or, to use traditional Reformed or Presbyterian language, we are set free to use the life of the mind in the service of God. As Daniel L. Migliore succinctly concludes: "Christian faith is thinking faith."[1]

In more practical terms for contemporary persons perhaps, the biblical understanding of faith means that there is no necessary conflict between the claims of science and the claims of the Christian faith. It is telling that the church often loses people at precisely the age when they arrive at the point of critical thinking–late adolescence or early adulthood. Having been taught the methods and results of critical thinking in high school or college–in fields like biology, chemistry, physics, geology, and astronomy–young persons have trouble assessing these learnings in light of their experiences in church, where they have generally been offered no encouragement or help in thinking about God. Most often young persons have apparently concluded that the church with its God-talk is naive, outdated, or simply wrong. These conclusions can be avoided if the church would adhere to the biblical understanding of faith as trust, thereby freeing people to confront honestly and openly their many questions, and thus freeing them to think about God.

From this perspective, thinking about God is a form of witness; and, as we suggested in the Introduction, we are concerned in this book with how popular songs serve as a witness to the Gospel. To be sure, there are not many songs that explicitly invite us to think about God, as Dishwalla's "Counting Blue Cars" does. But there are several songs that explicitly mention God and thus at least implicitly invite us to think about God. In view of what has been said thus far, one should not expect these songs to represent detailed doctrinal statements or developed creedal formulations. To the contrary, the first four songs to be discussed in this chapter speak of God in untraditional and striking ways; God is depicted as tired and indecisive (Crash Test Dummies, "God Shuffled His Feet"), as needing help (Tori Amos, "God"), as having a feminine personality (Dishwalla, "Counting Blue Cars," which we shall consider further), and as "a stranger on the bus" (Joan Osborne, "One of Us"). The value of these portrayals of God is precisely their striking strangeness, which virtually forces us to think about God.

What Robert Coles says about stories applies at this point to these four popular songs and their value as a witness to the Gospel. According to Coles, "The whole point of stories is not 'solutions' or 'resolutions' but a broadening and even a heightening of our struggles."[2] In other words, the whole point of these four songs is that they evoke the questions that lead us to think about God. That they may leave us without "solutions" or "resolutions" is actually quite appropriate theologically. As William C. Placher has pointed out, one of the problems with theology in the modern era has been its propensity to make "regrettable claims to explain too much."[3] By stimulating us to think about God without claiming to have God all figured out, these four songs invite us to stand faithfully in the biblical tradition and the ecumenical theological tradition of the church.

As Placher also demonstrates, thinking about God without claiming to explain too much not only protects God's transcendence, but it also makes it possible to speak faithfully and meaningfully of crucial biblical and theological concepts like grace and love. If there is any "solution" or "resolution" that the Bible offers, it is the ultimately mysterious and inexplicable good news that God is essentially loving and that God treats a sinful world with unfailing grace. It is this good news that is highlighted in the final two songs discussed in this chapter, "For the Love of It All" by Noel Paul Stookey, and "Show The Way" by David Wilcox.

Reimagining God

As suggested above, human beings have always engaged in theology—thinking about God. Indeed, the production of the Jewish and Christian scriptures resulted precisely from the process of thinking about God. As Paul Achtemeier persuasively argues, to speak of the inspiration of scripture is to speak about a process of tradition, new situation, and response; in other words, Jews and Christians affirm that God was at work in a special way in a prolonged process essentially involving generations of people thinking about God.[4] Even those who argue that the canon of scripture is closed do not deny that the process of inspiration and God's revelation of God's self continued after the New Testament era. For instance, the doctrine of the Trinity, which Christians routinely affirm as an essential of their faith, was not fully developed and finally articulated until the fifth century A.D. This doctrine was developed as Christians struggled to express their conviction that Jesus of Nazareth fully incarnated the God of Israel; in other words, the doctrine of the Trinity was developed as persons continued to think about God and to struggle to articulate their thoughts. And this process has continued and still continues in the development of creeds and confessions, as well as in the deliberations and pronouncements of church councils and assemblies. To use a term that has become popular in recent years, what the church has been and is constantly about is reimagining God.

To be sure, the notion of reimagining God has been not only popular but also controversial. It is easy to forget that scripture came into being through a process of humanity's thinking about its encounter with God, and it is easy to forget that this process of inspiration and revelation continued and continues. Many Christians in years past and still today unreflectively assume that to be God means essentially to be unchanging and unchangeable. After all, they point out, the Bible itself proclaims that God is "the same yesterday, today, and forever" (Heb. 13:8). What the Bible *means* by this, however is that God's essential character—that is, God's grace and love—never changes. But the Bible itself is the story of how God does change in terms of the strategies God uses to reach out to a wayward world and to respond lovingly toward sinful humanity. Indeed, the Bible very explicitly says that God changes God's mind (see Ex. 32:12–14).

Given this biblical way of thinking about God, it is surprising that the notion of an unchanging and unchangeable God became crystallized in the traditional understanding of what are known as "the classical attributes of God": God's omnipotence (all-powerfulness), omniscience (all-knowingness), and omnipresence (everywhereness). Particularly problematic in view of the actual biblical portrayal of God is the way in which God's omnipotence has traditionally been understood to mean that, because God is all-powerful, God does or is the cause of everything. The real problem arises when one places this traditional understanding of omnipotence alongside the biblical affirmation that God is good (Ps. 107:1; 118:1). If God is good and all-powerful, then what accounts for the reality of evil in the world? The problem is usually designated as theodicy (literally, "the justice of God"), since the justice of God appears to be nullified by evil in the world, including the suffering of the righteous and the prosperity of the wicked.

The problems surrounding the traditional understanding of God's omnipotence are compounded when this traditional understanding is accompanied by another notion that also appears to have some biblical support–the doctrine of retribution, which insists that God materially rewards the righteous and punishes the wicked. Pay careful attention to the dilemma–that is, if God rewards the righteous and punishes the wicked, and if an all-powerful God causes everything, then suffering must inevitably be interpreted as divine punishment! The book of Job explores this issue thoroughly; and Job's friends exemplify the logic of the doctrine of retribution when they conclude that the suffering Job is obviously being punished by God. The cruel corollary to this conclusion is that all afflicted persons deserve their afflictions, and the way is wide open for blaming the victims, thus victimizing them even further. For example, a frequently heard contemporary conclusion is that the poor obviously deserve to be poor, and if they'd just work harder, everything would be all right. To be sure, this conclusion may be sound in some cases; for in fact, some people are poor because they are lazy. But far, far more poor people work much harder than rich people, and they are poor for a number of very complex reasons (such as that our economy can produce and sustain only a certain proportion of high-paying jobs, or that there is discrimination against women and minorities). The extremely simplistic conclusion, that the poor deserve to be poor, allegedly supported on theological grounds, conveniently absolves the wealthy of any responsibility to help those less fortunate. Why should the prosperous help those whom God is punishing?

Such a position is rampant in North American society; it is held by many North American Christians, who apparently have no awareness of how utterly unbiblical it is! Indeed, Jesus directed a significant portion of his ministry to the poor and afflicted, not condemning them but rather embracing them with compassion. Such a response is in complete continuity with the God of Israel, whom Christians affirm that Jesus incarnated, a God who hears the cries of the afflicted and responds not with condemnation but with deliverance (see Ex. 3:7-8). The word "compassion" means literally "suffering with." If most Christians don't seem to have trouble with accepting compassion as a fundamental characteristic of God, then why do they seem to have so much trouble with the conclusion that therefore God suffers?

The answer seems to lie in the pervasive influence of the classical attribute of omnipotence. A suffering God just does not seem to be all-powerful. So, despite the evidence of God's suffering in the Old Testament, and despite even the suffering of Jesus (whom Christians profess incarnates God), most Christians still persist in concluding that God cannot suffer, and many further conclude that human suffering is evidence of God's punishment.[5]

To be sure, there is no easy "solution" or "resolution" to this basic theological issue. Unfortunately, therefore, the church has most often chosen not to struggle with the dilemma—that is, not to think about God. Rather, in an unthinking attempt to protect both God's omnipotence (as traditionally understood) and God's goodness, Christians have concluded that an all-powerful God cannot suffer or change, and furthermore that human suffering must be divinely willed punishment for human sinfulness. But the cost of these traditional conclusions is devastating! *Think* about it! A God who cannot suffer or change God's mind cannot really be a relational God, as the Bible affirms God to be. In other words, to use the Bible's own vocabulary, the concept of *covenant* is emptied of all real meaning. Furthermore, if God is locked into a system of rewarding and punishing human behavior, there is absolutely no room for crucial biblical concepts like grace and the forgiveness of sins. The irony is tragic. In its unthinking attempt to protect God's goodness and omnipotence, the church has actually portrayed God finally as distant, untouchable, and incapable of love, compassion, and grace!

There is an alternative. It does not claim to have God all figured out, but it does involve the advantage of actually thinking about God, and it is both simple and biblical. As opposed to the traditional understanding of God's omnipotence, the alternative affirms that God both suffers and changes! God does so because God has chosen to be in genuine relationship with humankind. Genuine relationship means above all that humanity is really free, including free to reject God. According to the Bible, this is precisely what happened (see Gen. 3), and this "original sin" has proven to be characteristic of humankind. Given the freedom to obey God, we consistently choose to disobey, focusing instead on our own selves and our own purposes. Because God cares for us, this disobedience and the accompanying destructive consequences (see Gen. 4, and the rest of the Bible, not to mention human history in general!) hurt God. That is, God suffers on account of our disobedience. It is also human disobedience that, in effect, forces God's hand. In other words, because humankind originally disobeyed and continues to disobey, God resorts to new and creative strategies to respond to humankind in an effort to reach and rescue God's wayward creatures. That is, God changes God's mind. A change of mind on God's part is implied as early as the opening chapters of Genesis (compare Gen. 6:5 and 8:21); God's change of mind is explicitly indicated in Exodus 32:12–14, and indeed, the unfolding of the biblical story involves new and creative strategies on God's part to get through to sinful humans.

What seems to bother people about this utterly biblical portrayal of God is that a God who suffers and changes appears to be weak and out of control. But the problem is more illusory than real. After all, only a truly strong being can really afford to be vulnerable. Because God is *infinitely strong,* God *can* remain in relationship with a humanity that consistently disobeys and hurts God. And because God *is infinitely loving* (and this is what never changes!), God *is willing* to remain in a relationship with humanity. It is precisely God's ability and God's willingness to love a sinful humanity that constitutes God's omnipotence, properly understood. In this alternative to the traditional understanding of God, omnipotence cannot be God's "control" of everything. By choosing genuine relationship with humankind, God has relinquished "control." Rather, omnipotence becomes God's ability to bear the sin and pain and brokenness of the world without being crushed by the incredible weight of it all. Just think of what an incredible all-powerfulness this kind of omnipotence represents! For instance, think about how you respond to personal disappointment or tragedy or setback. Or think about how you respond to a child's or parent's pain. If you're like most people, you tend to be "crushed" or "broken" by it, or you tend to "fall apart," or you may tend to withdraw, or give up all together, or resent those causing the pain. Now multiply your own personal and familial pain and disappointment by the billions of people in the world and you may begin to appreciate the incredible power of a God who bears the hurt, disappointment, and pain of the world without falling apart, without resentment, without giving up, and without failing to respond with love and compassion. Such is God's omnipotence, the incomprehensible ability and willingness to love the whole world!

If the ability and willingness to love the whole world means that God suffers (and it does!), then such suffering is to be seen not as a sign of weakness but of ultimate strength. If the ability and willingness to love the whole world means that God makes God's self vulnerable to human disobedience (and it does!), then such vulnerability is to be seen not as a weakling's last resort but rather as the ultimate act of generosity by a confident sovereign who is not afraid to appear to be weak.

The reality of a God who suffers and changes because of an unchanging and unfailing love for the world alters, of course, the traditional approach to the problem of theodicy. If omnipotence no longer means control, then the existence of evil and suffering in the world can logically be laid at the feet of humanity rather than God. Suffering, or at least much of it, can be attributed not to God's design nor God's will, but rather to the sinful choices of humankind and the destructive effects of these choices. Then too, if suffering is not antithetical to divinity, some suffering can be attributed simply to the conditions of creatureliness.[6] In any case, suffering cannot unthinkingly be attributed to God's will nor to God's activity to punish the wicked. Indeed, suffering and evil cannot be easily equated. The afflicted are liberated from blaming themselves, and the prosperous can no longer congratulate themselves for their good fortune or blame victims for being poor or afflicted. The doctrine of retribution is obliterated, and space is created for the existence of grace and compassion.

Indeed, one could say that knowledge of a loving, gracious God, who wills unending relationship with humankind and is willing to suffer for the sake of this relationship, creates a whole new world! In fact, this is exactly what Jesus said; he called this new world "the reign of God," and he invited people to live in it (Mk. 1:14–15). Because this new world is based on grace and love, not merit and control, everyone is welcome in it. In a world where the doctrine of retribution has been obliterated, there is even a special place for the humbled, the humiliated, the poor, the grieving, the meek, and the persecuted. Jesus went out of his way to welcome these kind of folk; and he announced that these kind of folk, often construed as victims, were to be welcomed as the fortunate or "happy" (see especially the two versions of the Beatitudes in Mt. 5:1–13 and Lk. 6:20–22).

As people often respond when reading the Beatitudes, "That's not the real world!" And they are correct, of course. The new world of God's reign is anything but the world of business, politics, and religion as usual. That "real world" is based primarily on merit and control. Suffering is to be avoided at all costs. The value of people is measured not in terms of genuine relatedness, but rather in terms of what they can do for me and to further my success. Jesus had the audacity to announce that the so-called "real world" is not real after all. The *real* "real world," as we like to call it, is the world of God's reign. As Jesus said and demonstrated, the *real* "real world" is grounded in grace, compassion, and love. The God who undergirds it is a suffering sovereign, one whose infinite strength means the freedom to be vulnerable, and one whose infinite love means the freedom to suffer.

While North Americans have always been and remain a very religious people, we need to address the question of *what kind of God* we believe in. In contrast to the traditional construal of God's omnipotence as control or sheer force, our rethinking or reimagining of God construes God's omnipotence as compassion (literally, "suffering with") or sheer love. Reference to popular songs will illustrate this direction and some of its implications as we continue the discussion of God's character. In short, songs will help us listen further for God and think further about God.

The Vulnerable God
(Crash Test Dummies, "God Shuffled His Feet")

The song "God Shuffled His Feet" by the Crash Test Dummies starts where Scripture starts–with creation. Although it doesn't actually use the word, the song is a sort of imaginative reflection on the meaning of Sabbath (see Gen. 2:1–3). This is evident from the opening two lines, which suggest that after creating the world, God is "quite tired." The value of these opening lines is that they make us think about God in a new way. We have probably heard for years, as Genesis 2:2 states, that "God rested on the seventh day." And we have probably never realized that Genesis 2:2 at least implies that God was "quite tired"! We have probably never thought about God in this way, because we have been influenced by the traditional understanding of omnipotence, as discussed earlier. A God who is all-powerful, in terms of control, should not get "quite tired." Thus, "God Shuffled His Feet" pushes us to rethink the traditional understanding of God, and it moves us in the direction of God's vulnerability. The creation of the world cost God something. The establishment of a situation in which God and humankind could exist in partnership was a great risk for God. The free human beings could prove to be unworthy partners. As suggested earlier, this is exactly what happens in the biblical account (Genesis 3). This outcome is also implied in "God Shuffled His Feet," in which the human beings refuse to enjoy the picnic that God has prepared. Instead, they ask rather trivial questions of God (not unlike those Jesus' opponents asked him in the Gospels; see, for example, Mt. 22:23–28); and upon not receiving a satisfactory answer, all they can manage to do is sit and stare at God. God is reduced to feet-shuffling and to staring back at the people. Thus, the song implies God's disappointment at the people's lack of appropriate response. As Terence Fretheim suggests of the biblical account, "The very act of creation thus might be called the beginning of the passion of God."[7] In other words, God made Godself vulnerable and opened God's self to suffering by creating human beings who could (and would) refuse to honor their relationship with God.

"God Shuffled His Feet" also helps us to arrive at the deeper meaning of the Sabbath. To be sure, it was intended for people (and God!) when their work had made them "quite tired," but it was more than this. The cessation of work was meant not only to provide time to re-energize, but it was also meant to offer the opportunity to enjoy and nurture the human relationships that God had built into the creation. In Jewish households, for instance, the Sabbath still begins with a festive meal, and it is enjoined upon Jewish couples to enjoy sexual intercourse on the Sabbath. The enjoying and nurturing of relationships is a dimension of the Sabbath that "God Shuffled His Feet" captures very well. In the song,

God sets aside a day for picnics, and God provides people everything that is necessary for a good picnic. The apparent purpose of the picnic, complete with bread and wine (a possible allusion to Passover and the Lord's Supper), is that God and human beings might enjoy one another's presence.

But this doesn't happen in the song any more than it happens in the biblical account. Instead, the people pester God with silly questions. Not only is God apparently disappointed, as suggested earlier, but God is also genuinely perplexed at the people's inability or refusal simply to enjoy the picnic, to enjoy God and one another. This seems to be the sense of the line that forms the title of the song and part of the refrain: "God Shuffled His Feet." As Fretheim has pointed out, God's frustration and perplexity over the people's refusal to respond appropriately is a regular feature of the Old Testament. It is present at the beginning of the Bible when Adam and Eve refuse to be content in Eden; it is present in the Sinai narratives when the people almost immediately break the covenant that God has established with them (see Ex. 32–34); and it is evident in the prophetic books, especially Jeremiah and Hosea, where God regularly expresses surprise, frustration, and hurt at the people's abandonment of the covenant relationship (see Jer. 3:7, 19–20; Hos. 6:4; 11:8–9).[8] This surprise, frustration, and hurt express what it means for God to be vulnerable.

Humanity's lack of an appropriate response to God is evident not only in "God Shuffled His Feet" and throughout the Old Testament, but it is also a feature of the New Testament. Jesus described the reign of God as a banquet—in essence, a big party (not unlike a picnic, complete with bread and wine!) thrown by God to which all are invited (see Mt. 22:1–10; Lk. 14:12–24; see also the discussion of Kevin Kinney's "Shindig With the Lord" in chapter 3). But when Jesus spoke about the reign of God in this way, he inevitably pointed out that most folk refused to join God's party. Indeed, the opposition to Jesus and his ministry, and Jesus' eventual crucifixion, are the culmination of the theme that begins in Genesis 3—the refusal of humankind to respond appropriately to God's offer of the kind of relationship that means abundant life. Jesus' crucifixion is an indication that God's vulnerability has become God's suffering.

The Suffering God (Tori Amos, "God")

The vulnerability of God already suggests that God suffers, and Tori Amos' song titled "God" assists us to think further about the dimensions of and reasons for God's suffering. As is often the case, Amos' lyrics have the appearance of a stream-of-consciousness flow, making them difficult to follow. The refrain to "God," however, is clear and it is on the refrain that we shall focus:

> God sometimes you just don't come through.
> God sometimes you just don't come through.
> Do you need a woman to look after you?
> God sometimes you just don't come through.

Amos' observation that God doesn't "come through" seems to be grounded in the traditional approach to the issue of theodicy (see earlier discussion). That is, because God is supposed to be both in control and good, bad things should not happen, at least not to good people. When they do, according to the traditional approach, then God has not "come through" and thus apparently needs some help.

We have attempted earlier in this chapter to dismantle the traditional approach to theodicy and to God, and thus we do not find Amos' starting point helpful. Her focusing of attention on God's possible neediness, however, is helpful, and it can be taken as a stimulus to make us think how and why we may legitimately speak of God as needing someone. In short, the question is this: If God does not need help as a result of God's failure, then how and why might God need someone?

The answer to this question, though a profound mystery, is quite simple: God is love! (1 Jn. 4:8). Because the God revealed in the Bible is essentially and unfailingly loving, this God, to be true to God's own character, cannot exist in isolation. This God is inevitably relational, or in biblical terms, covenental. In this sense, God always needs an object of the divine love–humanity, the world, the whole creation.

With a little poetic imagination, one might even borrow Amos' words to ask God: "Do you need a woman to look after you?" For in a real sense, God does need another someone. The need is not for someone to pick up after God's failures, as Amos suggests. Rather, the need involves simply the dynamics of loving and being loved.

The essential lovingness and inherent communality of God are what the church has historically affirmed by way of the doctrine of the Trinity. As a mathematical formula, the Trinity is nonsense. Everyone knows that one is not three, and three is not one. But as a theological formulation, the Trinity is full of meaning. It affirms that, even considered apart from any other someone who might be the object of the divine love, God is still essentially loving and communal. The Godhead itself is a triune community, characterized not by hierarchy but by the mutuality of shared love. Another poet, Brian Wren, captures well this dimension of the Trinity in two lines that begin the first two verses of one of his hymns. First, "God is one, unique and holy." Second, "God is oneness by communion, never single or alone."[9] To be "Never single or alone" suggests that, in an important sense, God always needs someone. Or more, simply, God is love.[10]

People generally resist so strongly the association of need with God because they work out of the traditional understanding of God's omnipotence, and need implies weakness and insufficiency. In North American culture, to need other people is a sign of immaturity, even a lack of mental health. In fact, the therapeutic community has taught us to call the condition of needing other people *co-dependency*, a decidedly negative evaluation. But recently, therapist Mary Pipher has rethought this matter. As she points out, needing other people is not a sign of weakness but of strength, a positive sign of mental health. She suggests, therefore, that we call co-dependency by the name it used to be known—namely, love![11] The doctrine of the Trinity affirms that God is fundamentally co-dependent; in short, God is love.

What then do we say about Amos' perception that God does not "come through"? According to our reimagining of

God, the suffering that indicates to traditional eyes the failure of God is more likely to result from the failure of human beings to be worthy partners of God and each other. To be sure, God is hurt by such human suffering, because God loves the world. Plus, another layer is added to God's suffering when we blame God for hurtful wrongs and injustices for which we humans ourselves are responsible. From this perspective, God might welcome a few human defenders of the divine reputation—in Amos' terms, a woman to look after God's cause.

A final observation can be made about Amos' choice of a woman to look after God. We don't know exactly what she had in mind, of course, but the line from her song reminds us of Jesus' suffering and of the gender of the few who actually looked after him in his hour of need. Completely abandoned by the male disciples, Jesus was at least attended to from afar by the women who followed him (see Mk. 15:40–41; note that Mk. 15:41 specifically states that these women had formerly "provided for" Jesus). Then too, it was an unnamed woman who performed for Jesus the service that his disciples should have provided—the preparation of his body for burial (Mark 14:3–9). Here again, it is a woman who, in essence, looks after God!

It is possible too that Amos intended to indicate the inadequacy of speaking about God in exclusively masculine terms, a concern that she has articulated in public interviews (see also her song "Muhammad My Friend," on the CD titled *Boys for Pele*). In any case, this concern is one to which we now turn.

The God of Motherly Compassion
(Dishwalla, "Counting Blue Cars")

At the beginning of this chapter, we focused on the subtitle of Dishwalla's "Counting Blue Cars" as an invitation to think about God. The lines which follow "Tell me all your thoughts on God" suggest a specific direction for thinking about God, one that is particularly precious to some persons and especially challenging to others. At several points in the song, these lines suggest that the singer wants to meet God, wants to ask God about human identity, and is even on his way to visit her. In short, the song speaks about God in feminine terms rather than masculine, and many would suggest that this is the primary theological value of the song. For instance, in an article that urges the church to take seriously the music of the younger generations, Jay Hudson observes:

> The repeating refrain in Dishwalla's "Counting Blue Cars" from the *Pet Your Friends* album is, "Tell me all your thoughts on God, 'cause I'd really like to meet her." It offers a gentle confrontation to the patriarchal church, suggesting that if God is beyond gender distinctions, then maybe, I would like to meet her and, "Ask her, why we're who we are." Dishwalla captures a spiritual longing that seems to get turned off by the church's limited view of God.[12]

We agree! In fact, we've been suggesting throughout this chapter that we all need to rethink "the church's limited view of God." Almost certainly the church's refusal to think of God in terms of vulnerability and suffering–that is, as an essentially loving God–is linked to the overwhelming propensity to think of God in exclusively masculine terms. Rather than shaping our notions of appropriate power in terms of a vulnerable, suffering, loving God, we have imagined God's power in terms of the traditional characteristics and roles of the Western male–dominant, in control, tough, unemotional, self-sufficient, independent. Given the apparent propensity to create God in our image rather than to shape ourselves upon God's image, it is all the more important that we reimage or reimagine God in feminine as well as masculine terms.

It is important to realize that this endeavor is not the recent invention of the women's movement. In fact, the Bible itself leads the way! Although it is true that masculine images for God are predominant in scripture, reflecting the Bible's origin in a highly patriarchal culture, there are a surprisingly large number of feminine images for God that occur in crucial places. Two examples must suffice.

The first occurs at the culmination of the crucial golden calf episode in Exodus 32–34. After the exodus (Ex. 1–15) and after God has given the people the Ten Commandments on Mount Sinai (Ex. 20), there is a covenant-sealing ceremony on the mountain, as a part of which the people promise twice to be obedient to all that God has spoken (Ex. 24:3, 7). The very next time that the people speak, however, they command Aaron to make idols (the golden calf) for them to worship, thus immediately breaking at least the first two of the Ten Commandments (Ex. 32:1). To put it mildly, God is furious, and God vows to destroy the people and start over with Moses (Ex. 32:7–10). Interceding for the people, Moses talks God out of this plan, and "the LORD changed his mind about the disaster that he planned to bring on his people" (Ex. 32:14).

To use theological terms, it is Moses' will and not God's will, at least as God originally stated it, that is done! Here God is strong enough to be vulnerable; God is open to Moses' leading. And by changing the announced divine plan, in essence forgiving the people, God takes upon God's own self their sin; in short, God suffers. While there is some unevenness to the narrative, it is crucial to note that the whole golden calf episode culminates with a proclamation about God's character:

> The LORD, the LORD, a God merciful and
> gracious, slow to anger, and abounding in steadfast
> love and faithfulness. (Ex. 34:6)

This proclamation becomes a sort of brief confession of faith that occurs throughout the Old Testament (Neh. 9:17, 31; Ps. 86:15; 103:8; 111:4; 145:8; Joel 2:13; Jon. 4:2), but for our purposes at this point, it is especially important to note that the first characteristic of God, "merciful," involves a Hebrew word that points in a decidedly feminine direction in describing God. The Hebrew word is *rahûm*, an adjectival form related to a noun that means "womb." Thus, Phyllis Trible suggests that we translate the characteristic of God described by *rahûm* as "motherly-compassion."[13] God loves and is bound to God's wayward children like a faithful, unfailing mother. In any case, by virtue of the appearance of *rahûm* in Ex. 34:6 and throughout the Old Testament, the

Bible's portrayal of God is inherently feminine as well as masculine.

The second feminine imaging of God occurs in material growing out of the greatest crisis confronting God's people in the Old Testament, the Exile. The northern kingdom was destroyed in 722 B.C.E., the southern kingdom followed in 587 B.C.E.; and the people articulated the conviction that their existence as God's people had come to an end. Virtually every voice in the Old Testament responds directly or indirectly to this crisis, but one of the most articulate is the unnamed prophet of the Exile whose words are preserved in Isa. 40–55. Given the people's perception that they had been completely abandoned by God on account of their sinfulness, the prophet appropriately responds by speaking of God and God's relationship to the people in the most intimate of terms. Not only is God the cosmic creator, but God is also the people's "redeemer," better translated "next-of-kin," which conveys the intimacy of the term (see Isa. 41:14; 43:14; 44:6, 24; etc.). Given the prophet's use of intimate family imagery, it is significant that Isaiah 40–55 contains the most consistent imaging of God in feminine terms. In direct response to the people's articulation of having been forsaken (Isa. 49:14), the prophet illustrates God's love for the people with the example of a nursing mother:

> Can a woman forget her nursing child, or show no compassion for the child of her womb? Even these may forget, yet I will not forget you. (Isa. 49:15)

Here God is not portrayed as faithful father, an image we may be more accustomed to, but rather as a faithful mother. Not surprisingly, the Hebrew word translated "compassion" is related to the word *rahûm* (see above). Above all, proclaims the prophet, God is a God of motherly compassion (see also Isa. 42:13–14; 45:9–13; 66:13).[14]

Dishwalla, whether aware of it or not, have appropriated this understanding of God's motherly compassion when they refer to God in feminine terms. By inviting us to think about God in feminine terms, they provide a way to imagine God that complements and fills out the portrayal of a vulnerable, suffering God.

Love Incarnate: God as "One of Us"
(Joan Osborne, "One of Us")

The first line of Joan Osborne's song "One of Us" explicitly raises the question of the character of God: "If God had a name, what would it be?" Especially in biblical terms, the word "name" suggests "character," "essence," or "reputation." In other words, what does God look like?—not so much in physical terms but in terms of character.

Actually, however, even the physicality of God cannot be avoided. The danger here, of course, is the risk of reducing God simply to human terms. Perhaps this danger has already occurred to readers of the previous sections; that is, how is a God who is vulnerable and who suffers anything other than simply human? The question and the concern are legitimate. We do not intend to reduce God to human terms. Our affirmation is that indeed God *is* omnipotent, all–powerful; but we want to be faithful to the biblical tradition that describes God's all-powerfulness not as sheer force but as sheer love. God is love! And God is God, because unlike human love, God's love never fails.

It is finally the Bible itself that makes us think about the physical side of God, and Osborne's questions sharpen the issue, especially the questions that form the refrain:

What if God was one of us?
Just a slob like one of us?
Just a stranger on the bus,
    trying to make his way home?

Osborne poses the issue in the form of questions. It is the Bible that affirms that indeed, God is one of us! The key text is Jn. 1:14, "And the Word became flesh and lived among us." This affirmation is known as the incarnation, literally, the *enfleshment.* In a fundamentally important way, the Bible affirms, God became one of us.

To be sure, the danger of misinterpretation is very real, and the presence of ambiguity is inevitable (see the Introduction). In our view, the incarnation does *not* simply reduce God to human terms, *nor* does it affirm that every human being is God, as some New Age movements seem to suggest. Rather, the incarnation affirms that God's life is intimately and inevitably bound up with human life and the life of the world. In short, God is essentially relational or covenantal, or even more simply, God is love. The incarnation affirms that in Jesus Christ, we see what God looks like, and what we see is essentially the fullness "of grace and truth" (Jn. 1:14). "Grace and truth" are the New Testament equivalents of "steadfast love and faithfulness," which occur in God's self-revelation to Moses in Ex. 34:6 in conjunction with *rahûm*, "motherly compassion" (see earlier). In John's Gospel, and in the others as well, Jesus lives out in human form the unfailing grace, compassion, and love of God. He is constantly opposed as a result (that is, his revelation of God makes him *vulnerable* to the political and religious establishment), and this opposition leads finally to his crucifixion (that is, Jesus *suffers*). And, as the Gospel of John puts it, "Whoever has seen me has seen the Father" (14:9). In other words, Jesus is God incarnate; Jesus shows us what God looks like.

To be sure, there is no "explanation" for the mystery of the incarnation, no "proof" in the scientific sense. The only proof that Christians can offer is their lives as transformed by the loving God.[15] And, of course, this is an ambiguous proof, since the church often does not act very Christlike (see Introduction). Perhaps the best "explanation" of the incarnation is the one in John's Gospel: "God so loved the world that he gave his only Son" (Jn. 3:16). The good news is that God became one of us, simply because God loves the world. God is love! And Jesus is love incarnate.

For those who trust this good news, there are profound and life-changing consequences. The video of "One of Us" brings to mind one of the most important of these consequences. As Osborne sings her questions, the video depicts a series of all kinds of people—different sizes, different ages, different colors, with different styles of dress and hair—taking their turn putting their faces in a wooden cut-out patterned after Michelangelo's paintings of God. The effect is powerful. It is apparently meant not to suggest that each of these persons is God, but rather that by taking on human flesh, God honored the whole human race, and thus God loves *all* these people in all their bewildering variety. If God loves *everybody*, the consequences are profound. No persons and no race or class of people can be dismissed, demeaned, disparaged, and discriminated against by those who claim to follow Jesus Christ.

There is no doubt that the church has often not grasped the full significance of this consequence. It has demeaned, disparaged, and discriminated against all kinds of people over the years—Jews; women; people of different races, classes, and sexual orientations—and it still does. The church's behavior is testimony to the difficulty of really believing that God loves the whole world. We are quick to believe that God loves *me* or *us*, but we are reluctant to believe that God loves *everybody*. This reluctance constitutes, in essence, a failure to believe in the grace of God. As Elsa Tamez suggests, if we really believed in God's grace, the consequence would be a pervasive sense of gratitude for the gift of life and a radical humility that would result in solidarity among all persons and classes of people.[16] Instead, by insisting on merit instead of focusing on grace, the church often fosters greed, encourages self-righteousness, and erects barriers between persons and classes of people. It would be different, and thankfully it *is* different sometimes and in some places, when Christians live out what the incarnation affirms—that God has become one of us, because God so loves the whole world.

The CD version of "One of Us" is preceded by a brief poem that is not included in the video version and that serves to highlight a different but related consequence of trusting the good news that God loves the whole world. The poem is as follows:

> One of these nights at about twelve o'clock
> This old earth's gonna reel and rock
> Saints will assemble and cry for pain
> For the Lord's gonna come in his heavenly airplane.

The purpose of the poem is to articulate a particular type of eschatology (which means literally, "a word about final things") usually known as apocalyptic. It envisions the cataclysmic end of the world as a result of God's intervention, and it is often associated with the second coming of Christ. Apocalyptic eschatology is pervasive among some groups of Christians, and its effect is to promote a very negative view of this world and its possibilities. In other words, it tends to promote the view that God actually hates this world, will someday (often seen as very soon) destroy it, and will take the good people (*not* everybody!) to a better world.

Osborne apparently chose this poem to indicate what her song is reacting *against.* In contrast to the view that God hates the world and will soon destroy it, Osborne offers the view that God loves the world so much that God has chosen to incarnate the divine self in the world. In this view, to destroy the world would be to destroy an important aspect of God's own self. In short, Osborne offers an alternative eschatology, and not surprisingly, it is an eschatology that is congruent with that found in the Gospel of John.

It is true that some portions of the New Testament support the notion of the second coming of Christ, but it is important to realize that *not all portions* of the New Testament do, and the Gospel of John is the crucial exception. As Robin Scroggs points out, in John the Holy Spirit represents the ongoing presence of the enfleshed Word (*Logos*) in the church and thus in the world. The logical consequence is that Christ cannot come again, *because Christ is already here!* For John, the gift of the Spirit on Easter evening (20:19–23) *was* the second coming of Christ.[17]

As it turns out, therefore, the eschatology Osborne offers in "One of Us" has a thoroughly biblical grounding in the Gospel of John. God will not send Jesus again to destroy the world, because God loves the world and because Christ is already here. John's eschatology, which offers an alternative to the apocalyptic eschatology of other parts of the New Testament, is the one that we find most compelling. It is compelling because it is consistent with the whole of the Bible, especially with the Bible's pervasive affirmation that God has chosen to be intimately and inevitably bound up with human life and the life of the world. Thus again, there is an important consequence of believing that God loves the world. It is to stand over against those who suggest that God actually hates the world and is out to destroy it. What is so frightening about the proponents of apocalyptic eschatology is that they actually seem to welcome and even encourage hatred and hostility among peoples and nations, because they are fond of interpreting such activity as part of their timetable for the end of the world. As we approach the year 2000, the end of one millennium and the beginning of another, the voices of the apocalypticists will grow louder and louder. Consequently, those who trust the good news that God loves the world will be called upon to stand over against them and their world-hating rhetoric. What we will want to say is something like what Osborne says in her song—that we know God loves the world and wills its future, because God has chosen to become "one of us."

For the Love of It All (Noel Paul Stookey, "For the Love of It All," and David Wilcox, "Show the Way")

The final two songs to be discussed effectively summarize the direction of the entire chapter: God is love (1 Jn. 4:8). The heading above is actually the title of a song written by Noel Paul Stookey (of Peter, Paul, and Mary; it is on a CD titled *PP&M (& LifeLines)*. The song is explicitly Christian, and it blends allusions to the Bible and allusions to recent history to offer a sort of interpretation of history grounded in the affirmation that God is love.

The song begins with the same words that open the Bible, "In the beginning," and after a brief poetic summary of Gen. 1, the song affirms that creation was fashioned by "The Love of It All" (see earlier discussion on "God Shuffled His Feet"). This line will subsequently serve as a refrain, ending each stanza of the song. With its references to "the tree," "forbidden fruit," and "the fall," the second stanza is a poetic interpretation of Genesis 3. In a way congruent with our discussion of theodicy, the song attributes the origin of evil not to God or to the serpent (which Christian tradition has often mistakenly identified with the devil), but rather to humanity itself:

One thing was clear; we chose not to hear
The Love of it all

Biblical and theological language and allusions continue in the next six stanzas, but they are interwoven with allusions to contemporary issues and events, such as the civil rights movement ("Gunned down on a highway," "I have a dream"), the environmental crisis ("Still the world is in labor,/She groans in travail./She cries with the eagle, the dolphin,/she sighs in the song of the whale"), and the peace movement ("And so we are marching to 'give peace a chance'"). Plus, there are calls to response and action, culminating in the final stanza:

For the Love of it all
We are gathered by grace.
We have followed our hearts
To take up our parts
In this time and place.
Hands for the harvest,
Hear the centuries call:
It is still not too late to come celebrate
The Love of it all.

The song ends with the following two lines, quoting Jesus' words from the cross (Mk. 15:34; see Ps. 22:1) after earlier having affirmed that "A man on a cross paid the ultimate cost: Eli, Eli, lemana shabakthani/The Love of it all."

The song does not actually use the word "God," but it is clear enough from its movement and content that "The Love" is its designation for God. By mentioning Jesus' cross and quoting his words from the cross, the song affirms that the origin and destiny of the world are grounded in the love of a God who has made God's self vulnerable to human disobedience and who is willing to pay the ultimate cost by suffering for the sake of God's unworthy human partners. Quite rightly, in our view, the song recognizes that it is precisely God's unfailing love that motivates God to be the vulnerable, suffering God of motherly compassion. Quite rightly too, and quite biblically, it also suggests that those who follow this God will share both God's glory and God's suffering (see Mk. 8:34-35; Rom. 5:1-5; 8:17). To return again to the Gospel of John, the peace experienced by God's followers will be "not as the world gives" (Jn. 14:27), but rather will be the gift of communion with God and reconciliation with one's brothers and sisters—in short, the opportunity "to come celebrate/The Love of it all."

Although quite different in conception and design, David Wilcox's "Show the Way" conveys much the same message as "For the Love of It All." Wilcox's metaphor for human life and the life of the world is an unfolding drama. The plot of this drama looks hopeless and evokes fear, since it appears that violence reigns ("'Cause there will always be some crazy with an Army or a knife"). But the outcome of the drama holds promise; it invites us to "play against the Fear," because finally the whole production has been staged by love. As the refrain puts it:

> In this scene set in shadows
> Like the night is here to stay
> There is evil cast around us
> But it's love that wrote the play...
> For in this darkness love will show the way

Note the similarities between "Show the Way" and "For the Love of It All." Neither song explicitly mentions God, but in both God is named by the word "love." Then too, while neither song is a theological treatise, both of them confront the issue of theodicy (see earlier discussion); that is, both acknowledge the reality of evil and violence as powerful forces in the world. Thus, for both songs, the love that names God is necessarily a vulnerable, suffering love. Rather than being hopeless or discouraged by love's apparent weakness, however, both songs are hope-filled invitations to action—"to come celebrate/The love of it all" and to "play against the Fear" and "against the reasons not to try."

The invitation issued by both songs might well be supported by the affirmation of 1 John 4:18 that "perfect love casts out fear." And, of course, for 1 John, as for Stookey and Wilcox, "God is love" (4:8). In the final analysis, then, Stookey and Wilcox are faithful to the Bible and to the church's theological tradition. When asked what his work as a theologian is really all about, David Tracy, one of today's leading theological thinkers, replied:

> The religious event described in the First Letter of John asks the question: What is the nature of ultimate reality? And the answer is: God. And, more explicitly, God is love. That is an extraordinary thought.
> This great mystery—that love *is* the basic reality. And that is what my work is all about.[18]

That love is the basic reality—this is also what the songs discussed in this chapter are all about, directly or indirectly. In facing the music, we find ourselves face-to-face with God. In listening to the sounds of our own culture, we are also listening for God.

NOTES

[1] Daniel L. Migliore, *Faith Seeking Understanding: An Introduction to Christian Theology* (Grand Rapids: Eerdmans, 1991), p. 5. In his discussion, "Theology as Faith Raising Questions" (pp. 2-5), Migliore cites Douglas John Hall, *Thinking the Faith: Christian Theology in a North American Context* (Minneapolis: Augsburg, 1989). For a helpful exposition of Paul's understanding of faith as trusting obedience, see Victor Paul Furnish, *Theology and Ethics in Paul* (Nashville: Abingdon, 1968), pp. 182-187. See also note 15.

[2] Robert Coles, *The Call of Stories: Teaching and the Moral Imagination* (Boston: Houghton Mifflin, 1989), p. 129.

[3] William C. Placher, *The Domestication of Transcendence: How Modern Thinking About God Went Wrong* (Louisville,Ky.: WJKP, 1996), p. 212.

[4] Paul J. Achtemeier, *The Inspiration of Scripture: Problems and Proposals*, Biblical Perspectives on Current Issues (Philadelphia: Westminster, 1980), esp. pp. 124-136. See also Johanna W. H. van Wijk-Bos, *Reimagining God: The Case for Scriptural Diversity* (Louisville: WJKP, 1995).

[5] For a thorough treatment of God's suffering in the Old Testament, see Terence Fretheim, *The Suffering of God: An Old Testament Perspective*, Overtures to Biblical Theology (Philadelphia: Fortress, 1984).

[6] See Douglas John Hall, *God and Human Suffering: An Exercise in the Theology of the Cross* (Minneapolis: Augsburg, 1986), pp. 53-62, where Hall argues persuasively that there was and is suffering apart from human disobedience. This suffering results from the conditions of creatureliness.

[7] Fretheim, *The Suffering of God*, p. 58.

[8] Ibid., pp. 45-46, 53-59.

[9] Brian Wren, "God Is One, Unique and Holy" in *The Presbyterian Hymnal: Hymns, Psalms, and Spiritual Songs* (Louisville: WJKP, 1990), No. 135.

[10] For helpful and more extended discussions of the Trinity in similar terms, see Migliore, *Faith Seeking Understanding*, pp. 56-79; and William C. Placher, *Narratives of a Vulnerable God: Christ, Theology, and Scripture* (Louisville, Ky.: WJKP, 1994), pp. 53-83.

[11] Mary Pipher, *The Shelter of Each Other: Rebuilding Our Families* (New York: G. P. Putnam's Sons, 1996), pp. 137-138. Pipher also recognizes, of course, that some relationships are "co-dependent" in a destructive way and need therapeutic intervention.

[12] Jay Hudson, "The Thirteenth Generation: Demographics and Worship," *Reformed Liturgy and Music* 30/2 (1996):47.

[13] Phyllis Trible, *God and the Rhetoric of Sexuality*, Overtures to Biblical Theology (Philadelphia: Fortress, 1978), pp. 31-56.

[14] See van Wijk-Bos, *Reimagining God*, pp. 50-65.

[15] For a helpful description of this kind of "proof," see Garrett Green, "Myth, History, and Imagination: The Creation Narratives in Bible and Theology," *Horizons in Biblical Theology* 12/2 (1990): 33. Green's discussion is also pertinent to the understanding of faith we have suggested in this chapter; see note 1 above.

[16] Elsa Tamez, *The Amnesty of Grace: Justification by Faith from a Latin American Perspective*, trans. Sharon H. Ringe (Nashville: Abingdon, 1993), esp. pp. 129-140.

[17] For this analysis of the Gospel of John, see Robin Scroggs, *Christology in Paul and John* (Philadelphia: Fortress, 1988), pp. 85-102.

[18] David Tracy, quoted in Eugene Kennedy, "A Dissenting Voice: Catholic Theologian David Tracy," *New York Times Magazine*, 9 November 1986, p. 31.

TWO

Facing the Music about Ourselves

Valuable and Vulnerable

Chapter 1 highlighted the basic biblical affirmation that God is love (1 Jn. 4:8). In other words, it is God's fundamental character to be relational, including relationship with humankind. The biblical affirmation that articulates the essential relatedness between God and humankind is that God created humanity in "the image of God" (Gen. 1:27). According to Paul Riceoer, "Each century has the task of elaborating its thought ever anew on the basis of that indestructible symbol [that is, "the image of God"] which henceforth belongs to the unchanging treasury of the Biblical canon."[1] In short, "the image of God" is a perpetual challenge to each generation to say how we understand who we are and how we understand the world in which we live. Chapter 2 attempts to take up this challenge. Whereas chapter 1 explored

41

what it means *for God and about God* to be related to human-kind, this chapter will explore what it means *for humankind* to be related to the kind of God whom the Bible reveals.

Beyond articulating the essential relatedness of God and humanity, "the image of God" points toward two basic affirmations that seem at first sight to be at odds with one another:

The Bible affirms that God has created humans to be genuinely free (see chapter 1). Only a free creature can par-ticipate in a relationship with integrity. In other words, only a free creature can love God and others, because love can-not be forced or programmed.[2] Beyond the freedom with which God has dignified humankind, the Bible affirms that God has also granted humankind "dominion over...every living thing that moves upon the earth" (Gen. 1:28; see Ps. 8:6–8). In effect, God has entrusted the care of the earth and its creatures to humankind. From the divine side, it is pre-cisely God's choice to establish a partnership with human-kind that makes God vulnerable to human failure and thus open to suffering (see chapter 1). But from the human side, God's choice highly exalts the human creature. As Ps. 8:5 puts it:

> Yet you have made them a little lower than God,
> and crowned them with glory and honor.

"Glory and honor" are attributes of sovereignty. On the one hand, then, by affirming that God has chosen to share God's sovereignty or power with humanity, the Bible offers a highly exalted view of the human and of humanity's vocation in the world.

On the other hand, the Bible honestly recognizes humanity's limitation and finitude. The same psalm that ar-ticulates humanity's "glory and honor" recognizes that in comparison to the vastness of the cosmos, the human crea-ture appears hardly worth noticing (Ps. 8:3–4). Furthermore, the Bible suggests that humanity's attempt to overstep its limits and reach beyond finitude resulted in the introduc-tion of sin and its destructive effects into God's good creation (Gen. 3). Human disobedience hurts God (chap. 1), and it also means that humans greatly multiply the suffering that may result simply from being finite and limited. That is, by disobeying God, humans also hurt each other.

Affirmation 1 and Affirmation 2 may be summarized by saying that the Bible affirms that humankind is both highly *valuable* and extremely *vulnerable*. The two affirmations are often seen as opposites, but their relationship would better be described as paradoxical. A paradox describes a situation in which two seemingly contradictory conditions are both true. In this case, the Bible offers as truth the affirmation that humankind is *both* valuable and vulnerable. Most people can readily see how the exalted status of humanity might image God, because most people seem to operate according to the traditional understanding of the classical attributes of God. In this view, when humans demonstrate themselves to be strong and powerful (in the sense of sheer force), then they are showing what God is like. But, when the classical attributes of God are rethought, as we suggested in chapter 1, then God's true power lies precisely in the unfailing love that makes God vulnerable to human failure and thus open to suffering. This rethinking means that humans image or represent God most clearly when they love. But since love means vulnerability and suffering, the further logical conclusion is that humans are also imaging God by way of their suffering! This conclusion reinforces the paradoxical rather than the contradictory relationship of Affirmation 1 and Affirmation 2. In other words, just as God's "'power is made perfect in weakness'" (2 Cor. 12:9), so is humanity's power. Properly understood, the phrase "the image of God" articulates this paradox.

The rest of the chapter will explore this paradox. Metallica's song and video, "One," will reveal an understanding of humanity that has clear resonances with the biblical phrase "the image of God." Failing to grasp the paradox results in a tragic misunderstanding of human status and vocation, as we shall suggest with reference to The Smashing Pumpkins and their song, "Bullet With Butterfly Wings." Two songs that do comprehend the paradox, especially when considered in juxtaposition, are REM's "Everybody Hurts" and Natalie Merchant's "Wonder." As these two songs suggest, a grasp of the paradox means an approach to the world and to human vocation that is both honestly realistic and essentially hopeful. This approach will be illustrated by the final two songs discussed in this chapter, Billy Joel's "You're Only Human" and Collective Soul's "The World I Know."

Love Is Life

Listening to and viewing Metallica's "One" requires some introduction, which a member of the group provides on the commercial video before the two versions of the song/video appear. The work is based on a book (later made into a movie) by Dalton Trumble titled *Johnny Got His Gun.* In the story, a young man goes off to World War I and is hit by mortar fire. Nearly totally annihilated, the young man is pronounced by doctors to be a living vegetable. But unbeknownst at first to the doctors, the young man still retains consciousness. Having had his face blown away, he cannot hear or talk, but he can think, and the story hinges on his thoughts and his attempts to communicate with other human beings.

In the "original main version" (7 minutes, 44 seconds), Metallica's song is accompanied by clips from the movie, in which the young man's thoughts can be heard. These thoughts replicate what may be identified as the basic human prayer: "Help!" At times, it is unclear whether the cry for help is addressed to God or to other humans; but at some points, the cry for help is clearly a prayer: "Oh God, please make them hear me…Oh please God, help me…help me…I need help!" Eventually, the attending doctors realize that the young man is trying desperately to communicate in Morse code by tapping the remains of his head on the bed. Decoders are summoned, and the communication again is "Help!" Only when the young man realizes that no attempt to achieve mutual communication will succeed does he tap out the message "Kill me," a request that amounts to the only help that he is in a position to receive because of his traumatic wounds.

The plot is tragic, but it is not hopeless, and Metallica has succeeded at their goal of producing a work of art that is "unique and different." The message is profound, and profoundly theological. The young man's problem was not really his pain or suffering, which must have been severe. Neither was his problem the fear of death. Rather, the overwhelming, indeed unbearable, problem was the inability to communicate. The message is clear. Human life is constituted by the ability to communicate, to relate, to speak—in short, to love. Love is life! The young man's desperate attempts to "speak" call to mind Walter Brueggemann's description of the human being, on the basis of his interpretation of "the image of God," as the "speech creature *par excellence.*"[3] Human beings image God precisely in their ability to speak, because communication is the fundamental prerequisite for relatedness—in short, for love! The inability to speak means alienation, which in biblical terms equals death.

The profoundly biblical direction of the message of Metallica's "One" is especially important in the kind of culture that characterizes most of North America. If genuine human life is constituted by relatedness to each other (not to mention God!), then we are missing it. Our culture systematically teaches us to be independent, self-centered, self-reliant—the very opposite of relatedness.[4] And increasingly, insofar as we do relate, it is with a television or computer screen or with people we don't have to face—"virtual reality," we call it, as opposed to *actual* reality or genuine relatedness. The danger is that the very technology that so enchants us is significantly *diminishing* our lives! Entertainment may mean enjoying ourselves, but life means loving other people, at least from the biblical point of view, a message reinforced by Metallica's "One."

A related danger of our cultural context is the pervasive message, especially from advertising and television, that pain and suffering are abnormalities to be avoided or denied at all costs. The effect is devastating. As Mary Pipher suggests, "Much of the terrible craziness in the world comes from running from pain."[5] Pain and suffering could and should be things that lead people to depend upon and help each other, but too often, especially among young people in our culture, they become sources of embarrassment, shame, isolation, alienation, and even suicide (see below). Recall that in "One," the self's problem is not the pain but the isolation. And recall that from the biblical point of view, humanity images God by way of its suffering, because a loving God is a suffering God (see above). In short, the good news is that pain is normative and that it can be endured, especially in a community that takes upon itself to "fulfill the law of Christ" (a form of imaging God!) insofar as it responds to the injunction to "bear one another's burdens" (Gal. 6:2). Elsewhere, Paul defines fulfilling the law as love (Rom. 13:10; Gal. 5:14). Love is life! The bad news, however, is that pain cannot be endured alone. Indeed, in the midst of a culture that promotes isolation and alienation, we are currently finding out firsthand how bad the bad news can be! To illustrate, we turn now to another song.

The Deadly Art of Pain Avoidance

The failure to understand that pain is a normal part of human life has disastrous consequences. To return to the terms used earlier, it means the inability to appreciate the *value* of human life because of human *vulnerability*. Instead of maintaining the paradoxical relationship between *valuable* and *vulnerable*, the two terms are seen as contradictions. To illustrate, we cite the song "Bullet With Butterfly Wings" by The Smashing Pumpkins. In the song, the singer's pain becomes the cause for concluding that "the world is a vampire." Not surprisingly, given this conclusion, the singer characterizes himself as a caged rodent—essentially isolated and without value. The song concludes with the singer's belief that salvation is not possible. In biblical terms, salvation means life. So, in other words, the singer's pain has caused him to conclude that life is impossible, or at least that it has no value or meaning.

Very perceptively, The Smashing Pumpkins recognize the relationship between two very important biblical characters whom they mention in their song—Job and Jesus. An exploration of these characters will reveal the possibility of a different way to view pain and suffering. Although apparently enraged at the emptiness or even impossibility of life, the singer vows to remain detached and cool like the biblical character Job. This reference to Job reveals the traditional misunderstanding of the book of Job and the character, Job, who did *not* keep his cool at all! In fact, only in chapters 1–2 of the book of Job, does Job keep his cool. After that, he explodes in rage and blasts God.

Interestingly, Job actually begins his response to intense pain and suffering in a way that is almost identical to the response of The Smashing Pumpkins. Because of his pain, he sees no value in life, wishes he had never been born, and longs to die (chapter 3). Job then begins a long and bitter conversation with his three "friends" and with God. Psalm 8, which we mentioned earlier, becomes a topic in the conversation. Because of the *vulnerability* of human life revealed by his suffering, Job denies the *value* of human life by alluding to and twisting the meaning of Ps. 8:4 (Job 7:17; see also 19:9). In other words, Job's pain leads him to deny the glory or value of human life that Psalm 8 affirms. In essence, Job sees himself as trapped, not unlike a caged rodent (see Job 7:1–6).

But unlike The Smashing Pumpkins, Job does not persist in his belief in the futility of life. Instead, in the midst of his suffering, Job gradually begins to realize that his pain does not represent punishment from God, and he begins to claim a dignity and a sense of integrity that pain cannot obliterate. Toward the end of the book, Job even declares that he is willing to confront God "like a prince" (31:37), thus reclaiming in the midst of his pain the exalted status of humankind that he previously had denied. In the last chapter of the book, after God has appeared and spoken, Job's change of mind is confirmed. The key verse is Job 42:6, which as opposed to the RSV, NRSV, and many other translations, should be translated as follows:

> Therefore I recant and change my mind concerning dust and ashes.[6]

What Job has recanted is his earlier conclusion that the vulnerability of human life makes it not worth living. He has changed his mind about the place and status of humanity, to which the phrase "dust and ashes" poetically refers (see Job 30:19; Gen. 18:27). Job now understands that human vulnerability does not devalue human life. He now understands that pain and suffering are normative. They are simply conditions for participation in creation, for both humanity and for God! In other words, Job now realizes that even as he suffers he is imaging God, because God also suffers with and for the sake of humankind.

As the book of Job unfolds, the reader has a big advantage over the character Job, because the reader knows from the outset that Job's suffering is not punishment from God. Rather, the whole plot of the book is set up so that Job's experience represents an opportunity *for God to learn* whether human beings can be faithful to God when they are not being rewarded or paid for it. The key question is voiced in Job 1:9 by the Satan, who must be understood in this context as something like God's investigative officer: "Does Job fear God for nothing?" In other words, the question is, from God's perspective, "Does Job really *love* me, or is he just loyal because he gets paid for it?"

When viewed from this crucial perspective, the key issue in the book of Job is love! A mechanistic reward-punishment scheme, which Job's three friends consistently defend (as did Job himself, at first), simply does not allow for genuine relatedness. By obliterating such a scheme, the book of Job affirms the fundamental relatedness of God and humankind. Love constitutes life! As the character Job demonstrates, suffering can be endured. What Job could *not* endure was the thought that God was his enemy. Even when he accused God of being an enemy (see 6:4; 9:17–18), Job's continuing conversation with God indicates an unbroken relatedness. And eventually Job realizes that God is on his side in the midst of the suffering (19:25–27), something that the reader has known all along.

The Smashing Pumpkins are correct to perceive a relationship between Job and Jesus. What Job demonstrates–

that suffering is not an indication of alienation from God, but that humanity actually images God by way of suffering–anticipates Jesus' life, death, and resurrection. Jesus, whom Christians affirm *incarnates* God (the ultimate in *imaging* God), was persistently opposed throughout his ministry. His suffering culminated in a cross, which proved to be a crown. For Jesus, suffering and glory were inseparable. The same is true for Jesus' followers, whom Jesus invites to "take up their cross" (Mk. 8:34). In other words, Jesus and his followers image God by way of their suffering!

From the biblical perspective, then, pain cannot mean that "the world is a vampire." Rather, suffering becomes a condition of life and of love. What The Smashing Pumpkins have failed to grasp is that to be vulnerable and to be valuable are *not* contradictory. Thus, they misinterpret Job and Jesus; they misunderstand themselves and the world; and they simply miss the essence of life, which is love. From this perspective, to try to avoid pain is nothing short of a deadly mistake.

Vulnerable and Valuable

We turn now to two songs that have grasped the biblical affirmation that humankind is both vulnerable *and* valuable: REM's "Everybody Hurts" and Natalie Merchant's "Wonder." REM emphasizes the vulnerable side of the paradox, whereas Natalie Merchant emphasizes the valuable side of the paradox, but both songs clearly succeed in maintaining the paradox, and they thus form a helpful pair.

"Everybody Hurts" is a case in which the video adds a great deal to the song (see Introduction). The song itself effectively makes the point that "Everybody hurts sometimes" and "sometimes everybody cries," but the video depicts the faces of hurting people, and its subtitles provide evocative interpretations of the pained faces: "Nobody can see me," "17 Years...," "She's gone," "There's nothing I can do." The poignancy and power of the depiction of vulnerability are increased by the setting of the video. The hurting people are in cars that are stalled on a freeway, perhaps the paramount symbol of contemporary isolation and alienation. Although hundreds or thousands of people may be present on a freeway at rush hour, there is no significant interaction among them. Or, if there is, it is "road rage" and not community.

While the song powerfully portrays the vulnerability of human life, it also clearly communicates how valuable life is. To those who are hurting, the counsel is to "Hold on," "Don't throw your hand" (that is, don't fold or give up), and "Take comfort in your friends." The video enacts this movement toward community when one of the hurting people gets out of his car, begins singing the advice not to give up, and invites others to join in: "Now it's time to sing along." The other hurting people get out of their cars and seem to form a community of support precisely in the midst of a place that symbolizes isolation. As suggested earlier, pain can be endured, but not alone. The video emphasizes this point. The line "If you feel like you're alone" is eventually answered by, "No, no, no, you're not alone."

The video even suggests a biblical and theological foundation for its depiction of the vulnerability and value of human life. On a flat-bed truck caught in the traffic jam, there is something that looks like a large crown of thorns. Another truck is transporting a green tree, perhaps symbolizing the tree of life. Together, these symbols communicate the inseparability of suffering and hope. One person lies in a cruciform shape on the top of his car, suggesting perhaps the cross, a symbol that for Christians communicates both suffering and hope. Another person oversees the whole scene from an overpass. He is reading a book, from which he tears pages that float to the pavement below, perhaps a symbol of the Word being proclaimed to bring vitality into what had appeared to be a hopeless situation.

While these symbols imply a biblical and theological foundation, the subtitles in the video make such a foundation very explicit. As pages of the book descend on the sufferers, the subtitles read as follows:

> Lead me to the rock that is higher than I.
> They that sow in tears shall reap in joy.

The first is a quotation of Psalm 61:2, and the second is Psalm 126:5. Both psalms are prayers for help, which are frequently labelled by scholars as psalms of lament or complaint. There are more prayers for help in the book of Psalms than any other kind, and they regularly give full articulation to hurt, pain, affliction, persecution, and oppression. But with one possible exception (Ps. 88), these psalms also express trust in God, and they celebrate the life that God promises and offers. The effect is to communicate both how vulnerable and how valuable human life is. Commenting on one of the prayers for help, Psalm 13, James L. Mays makes a point about all the laments:

> So in taking up the Psalm as our prayer, we are shown who we are when we pray. We are taught our true identity as mortals who stand on earth and speak to a God who is ours but never owned. Agony and adoration hung together by a cry for life—this is the truth about us as people of faith...
> The Psalm is not given us to use on the rare occasions when some trouble seems to make it appropriate. It is forever appropriate as long as life shall last. We do not begin at one end and come out at the other. The agony and the ecstasy belong together as the secret of our identity.[7]

Or, as Mays also suggests, the psalms of lament teach us this: "To be human is to desire life and rightness, and because we cannot autonomously secure either, to be essentially needy."[8] In essence, this is precisely what REM conveys with the message that "Everybody Hurts." The message is not an occasion for despair in either the Psalms or in "Everybody Hurts." In the Psalms, the neediness or vulnerability of human life impels people to take refuge in God. In "Everybody Hurts," the neediness or vulnerability may be an occasion to seek refuge in God (note the quote of Ps. 61:2; the next two verses of the psalm each mention "refuge"), but it is at least an invitation to "take comfort in your friends." In both cases, what is affirmed is both how vulnerable *and* how valuable human life is. The agony and the ecstasy belong together!

It was suggested earlier that one of the dangerous aspects of our culture is that it conveys the message that to hurt is abnormal. Especially among young people who have absorbed this message, pain becomes embarrassing and shameful. When this occurs, as "Everybody Hurts" recognizes, it is easy to "think you've had too much of this life." Often, the only way out seems to be suicide, and suicide is the third-leading cause of death among young people in the United States. Because the message of their song directly addresses this problem, REM has given permission for it to be used in national teen-suicide prevention campaigns. In a culture where self-centeredness promotes isolation and alienation, the message of "Everybody Hurts" is crucial: we are not alone. We have God– "the rock higher than I" (Ps. 61:2)– and we have each other. From the biblical perspective, which "Everybody Hurts" includes, "take comfort in your friends" could well be paraphrased "Bear one another's burdens" (Gal. 6:2). When we know we are not alone, then we can see that we are *valuable* even as we are *vulnerable*. Hurt can be endured when we are not alone.

While "Everybody Hurts" emphasizes the vulnerable side of the biblical paradox, Natalie Merchant's "Wonder" emphasizes the valuable side. Biblical language and imagery are again present, as the song affirms "I must be one of the wonders of God's own creation." The video deepens the meaning of this affirmation. It depicts not a single person singing the song, but rather it puts the song's repeated affirmation on the lips of a host of girls and women representing all ages, all races, and all nationalities. That human beings are "the wonders of God's own creation" is, in essence, what the Bible means by "the image of God" (Gen. 1:27; see above). The communal dimension is crucial, as the video suggests. Human beings image God not in isolation, but rather in community. In other words, the love that brings together persons of all ages, races, and nationalities represents who God is–God is love (1 Jn. 4:8; see chapter 1).

While "Wonder" affirms how *valuable* human beings are, it does not overlook human *vulnerability*. Unlike many music videos, this video depicts not just beautiful young women.

The women and girls in this video include those with physical and cognitive disabilities, those who are obviously weak and infirm, those who are middle-aged and elderly. The powerful message of the video is that physical weaknesses, the effects of aging, and disabilities do not make persons any less wonderful. In other words, these *vulnerable* persons are no less *valuable*.

In a real sense, the video depicts the kind of community that Jesus called the reign of God, in which the vulnerable were always valuable. In this regard, it is interesting to note that the singers of the song see themselves as "a challenge to your balance." The community of the vulnerable whom Jesus gathered was obviously a challenge to the traditional values of his society. This community, based on grace, erased distinctions among persons, and it amounted to what Paul called "a new creation" (2 Cor. 5:17). In any case, when one sees oneself and others fundamentally as "wonders of God's own creation," then that vision will profoundly affect how one relates to others and to the world, a dimension that we'll consider in the next section.

But first, one final word. While "Wonder" includes no men, its intent is not so much to exclude men as it is to advocate the equality of women. Unfortunately, such advocacy is necessary, because women have been and still are routinely devalued and discriminated against, in society at large and even as official policy in some Christian bodies.[9] Some theologians have even concluded that "the image of God" includes only maleness, despite the fact that the phrase, "the image of God," is followed in Genesis 1:27 by the statement that God created humankind "male and female." When this history of neglect and abuse is considered, then the video can be appreciated as an affirmation not only of women but of the value of all of us vulnerable human beings.

The World We Know

As suggested in the previous section, how we see ourselves as human beings affects how we view the world and our relationship to it. Unfortunately nowadays, how many people view life is shaped by television more than anything else. As Mary Pipher puts it:

> Most real life is rather quiet and routine...Television suggests that life is high drama, love and sex...Instead of enabling our ordinary experiences, television suggests that they are not of sufficient interest to document.[10]

As we have argued, and as Pipher points out too, ordinary experience includes pain and suffering. But if ordinariness, including pain and suffering, is seen as abnormal and problematic, then the world will tend to look like "a vampire," as The Smashing Pumpkins suggest in "Bullet With Butterfly Wings." Once one concludes that "the world is a vampire," human life is in danger.

The danger is illustrated in two final songs, Billy Joel's "You're Only Human (Second Wind)" and Collective Soul's "The World I Know." The premise of the two songs is similar, and the video in each case helps immensely in following the plot. In each one, a person is tempted to kill himself on account of the way he views life and the world. In "You're Only Human," a sixteen-year-old has wrecked his car, embarrassed himself in his neighborhood, and is in danger of losing his girlfriend. In "The World I Know," a young man is deeply troubled at the condition of the world—war, hunger, homelessness, and a seemingly pervasive alienation among people. In each case, the pain seems overwhelming. The teenager is poised to jump off a bridge, and the young man climbs a fire-escape in preparation to jump off a building. Both feel isolated. The teenager in "You're Only Human" feels as if he is the only person that has ever messed up, and he is described as isolating himself from others because of this feeling. The young man in "The World I Know" is aware of being all alone in a big city. As we suggested earlier, pain cannot be endured alone.

The resolution for each character comes in the form of a realization, or perhaps even a *revelation*, that he is *not* alone (see earlier on "Everybody Hurts"). In "You're Only Human," Billy Joel appears to the teenager as sort of an angel or messenger (which, in biblical terms, are the same thing) to show him what he will leave behind and what he will miss if he kills himself–a devastated family, the opportunity to complete school, the opportunity to marry. The messenger's refrain is the title of the song, "You're Only Human," and he interprets what being human means. It means that we *will* make mistakes that hurt ourselves and others. In other words, human life inevitably involves sin, pain, and suffering. What is needed, according to the messenger, is "a little faith" in order to "face the world again." It's this faith that the subtitle of the song represents as a "Second Wind," a sort of mysterious force that graciously imparts strength in moments of crisis. The messenger's role is to call this "Second Wind" to the attention of the teenager, who, having been shown a different vision of what it means to be human, chooses life.

In "The World I Know," the revelation comes when the despairing man extends his arms in a cruciform position as he stands on the ledge of the building. A dove alights on his hand, and a turning point occurs, signaled in the video by the transition from black and white to color. As he feeds the dove some crumbs from a bagel he retrieves from his pocket, the man is able to hear and see things he had overlooked before–to hear "hymns of offering" and to observe "that love is gathering." The man moves from feeding the bird to, in essence, feeding people as he begins to throw money (sometimes called "bread" or "dough") off the top of the building. Backing off from the ledge, he again assumes a cruciform position, but now he is laughing in celebration rather than crying in despair. The cruciform position seems intentionally symbolic; the cross, a symbol of death and despair, has become a symbol of life and the hope that the song had earlier suggested still persists amidst alienation. The world he knows has been transformed by the realization or revelation "that love is gathering," a reality that dispels loneliness and inspires a solidarity with others that is manifested as joyful generosity. This generosity answers the song's initial question concerning whether kindness has disappeared. Pain can be endured when we know we're not alone. When we know we're not alone, we can choose life.

There is explicitly biblical and theological language in the two songs–"faith," "hope," "hymns of offering," "love." Then too, the two pivotal symbols in the songs, wind and a dove, have biblical foundations and connotations. In fact, both are biblical symbols of God's "breath" or "spirit." In the Bible, God's breath or spirit is the creative force that makes life possible (Gen. 1:2; Job 33:14–15), and beyond that, the divine breath or spirit creates new possibilities for human life, especially in the way of creating community. Thus, in biblical terms, this spirit is Holy Spirit; it is responsible in the Book of Acts, for instance, for creating the church by uniting and empowering despairing and dispirited disciples (Acts 2), who went out and began "turning the world upside down" (Acts 17:6).

In other words, the world they knew was transformed, and so is the world we know transformed when we see it from the perspective of a God who is love. God's love motivates God to suffer with and for the sake of the world. From this biblical perspective, we humans image God by way of our suffering. Being *vulnerable* does not mean that we are not also *valuable*. The good news is that pain can be endured when we are "not alone." And the good news is that we are "not alone," because God is love, and "love is gathering" a community of kindness manifested in the mutual commitment to "love one another" (Jn. 15:12) and to "bear one another's burdens" (Gal. 6:2).

If there is any way that "the world is a vampire," it is that our culture pushes a logic of self-sufficiency, independence, and autonomy that results in alienation and its deadly consequences. The Bible offers a different world, what we called in chapter 1 the real "real world," the logic of which is love that results in life (see also chapter 3). The ancient choice that Moses posed for the children of Israel is remarkably contemporary. "I have set before you life and death, blessings and curses. Choose life so that you and your descendants may live" (Deut. 30:19).

NOTES

[1] Quoted on the frontispiece of Douglas John Hall, *Imaging God: Dominion as Stewardship* (Grand Rapids: Eerdmans, 1986).

[2] See Douglas John Hall, *God and Human Suffering: An Exercise in the Theology of the Cross* (Minneapolis: Augsburg, 1986), pp. 70–71.

[3] Walter Brueggemann, *Genesis*, Interpretation (Atlanta: John Knox, 1982), p. 31.

[4] See Mary Pipher's incisive analysis of contemporary culture in the United States in *The Shelter of Each Other: Rebuilding Our Families* (New York: G. P. Putnam's Sons, 1996), pp. 9–32 (see chapter 1, note 11).

[5] *Shelter*, p. 229.

[6] The translation is that of J. Gerald Janzen, *Job*, Interpretation (Atlanta: John Knox, 1985), p. 251.

[7] James L. Mays, "Psalm 13," *Interpretation* 34 (1980): 282.

[8] James L. Mays, *The Lord Reigns: A Theological Handbook to the Psalms* (Louisville, Ky.: WJKP, 1994), p. 54.

[9] For a thorough analysis of how girls and women are routinely devalued and discriminated against in our culture, as well as an assessement of the damage and a call to reform, see Mary Pipher, *Reviving Ophelia: Saving the Selves of Adolescent Girls* (New York: Ballantine Books, 1994).

[10] Pipher, *Shelter*, p. 90.

THREE

Facing the Music about Jesus

The End of the World as We Know It

In facing the music about God (chapter 1) and ourselves as humans (chapter 2), we have already had occasion to mention Jesus. It could hardly be otherwise, since the church's classical affirmation about Jesus is that he was both "fully divine" (chapter 1) and "fully human" (chapter 2). This christological formulation goes back to the Council of Chalcedon in the fifth century A.D. This may explain why it probably sounds to contemporary folk as if it were produced by a group of people who had flunked biology. How could Jesus be both "fully divine" and "fully human"?

Without claiming to exhaust the depth and mystery of the Chalcedonian formulation, suffice it to say that categories of thought have changed dramatically in the past 1,500 years. In other words, the Council of Chalcedon intended to make a *theological* affirmation about Jesus, not a *biological* assessment. What they affirmed, in essence, is that Jesus of Nazareth fully embodied what God wills for human life in the world. Jesus' life of perfect love *reveals precisely who God is,* so that Jesus can say in the Gospel of John 14:9: "Whoever has seen me has seen the Father." In short, Jesus was "fully divine." But Jesus' life of perfect love also *reveals precisely what God intends human life in all its fullness to be.* Jesus demonstrates authentic humanity. In short, Jesus was "fully human."

To be sure, the Chalcedonian formulation points to a God who has chosen to reveal God's self *incarnationally*–to be so fully related to and intimately involved with human life in the world that God ultimately *enfleshes* God's self. What we previously suggested that this means is extraordinarily simple: God is love! It is also simply extraordinary. That God is love means that God's power is manifest in the world not as sheer force but as sheer love (chapter 1). The consequences are revolutionary for God and for human life. Loving us and entrusting us with dominion of the earth, God opens God's own self to pain and disappointment. The good news is that God is both able and willing to bear the pain of the world. As for us humans, the good news is that our suffering does not indicate divine punishment nor does it separate us from God. Rather, our suffering becomes a crucial way in which we actually image God (chapter 2). For Christians, this good news is focused in Jesus, who was constantly opposed for being faithful to God and whose suffering culminated on a cross.

This revolutionary view of God and human life transforms the world, as we suggested at the conclusion of the previous chapter. And in this chapter, we shall explore further this affirmation. One could even paraphrase Jesus' proclamation of the reign of God as "The End of the World as We Know It," the title of a song by REM that we have chosen as the subtitle for this chapter and with which we shall begin. Jesus refused to accept the so-called "real world" as ultimately determinative, proclaiming instead the reign of

God, which we called previously the *real* "real world." We shall further explore the characteristics and dimensions of the world of God's reign with reference to two songs by Tracy Chapman, "Heaven's Here on Earth" and "New Beginning," that don't explicitly mention Jesus but that help us to appreciate the dynamics of the reign of God. Then we shall move to songs that are explicitly interpretations of Jesus' birth, ministry, death, and resurrection: Bruce Cockburn's "Cry of a Tiny Babe," The Dave Matthews Band's "Christmas Song," Kevin Kinney's "Shindig With The Lord," and Collin Raye's "What If Jesus Comes Back Like That."

Jesus' Proclamation of the Reign of God: The End of the World as We Know It

The Gospels of Matthew and Mark agree that from the very beginning of his public ministry, Jesus preached a very simple message: "The kingdom of God is at hand" (Mk. 1:15, NRSV note; see Mt. 4:17). In short, God reigns; the whole world is under God's claim. This basic message was accompanied by an invitation: "Repent, and believe in the good news" (Mk. 1:15). In other words, enter God's reign by submitting yourself to God's claim on your life and the life of the world.

In the Gospel of Matthew, the proclamation of God's reign is followed almost immediately by Jesus' teaching about the reign of God (Matthew calls it "the kingdom of heaven"). This section of teaching is known as the Sermon on the Mount. It begins with the Beatitudes (Mt. 5:3–11), in which Jesus proclaims certain people "blessed," "happy," or "fortunate"–"the poor in spirit," "those who mourn," "the meek," "peacemakers," even those who are persecuted for the sake of God's reign. As suggested in chapter 1, when contemporary North Americans hear the Beatitudes, their almost inevitable response is, "That's not the way things are in the *real world.*" What they mean is that in the so-called real world of business and politics and social arrangements as usual, the poor in spirit get taken advantage of, those who mourn are told to pull themselves together, the meek get trampled, peacemakers are told to get a life, and those persecuted for doing right are dismissed and ridiculed. And, of course, they are correct!

What this response fails to discern, however, is that Jesus claims to have inaugurated as a present reality a new and different world, which he called "the kingdom of God." In their discussion of the Sermon on the Mount (in a section titled "The End of the World"), Stanley Hauerwas and William Willimon describe Jesus' claim as follows:

> Jesus' teaching was not first focused on his own status but on the proclamation of the inbreaking kingdom of God, *which brought an end to other kingdoms.* His teaching, miracles, healings, indicate the nature and presence of the Kingdom. The Sermon on the Mount begins as an announcement of something God has done to change the history of the world. In the Sermon we see the end of history, an ending made most explicit and visible in the crucifixion and resurrection of Jesus. Therefore, Christians begin our ethics, not with anxious, self-serving questions of what we ought to do as individuals to make history come out right, because in Christ, God has already made history come out right. The Sermon is the inauguration manifesto of how the world looks now that God in Christ has taken matters in hand. And essential to the way that God has taken matters in hand is an invitation to all people to become citizens of a new Kingdom, a messianic community where the world God is creating takes visible, practical form.[1]

In other words, for those who accept Jesus' "invitation...to become citizens of a new Kingdom," the so-called "real world" is obsolete. They live in nothing short of a new world, which becomes the real "real world." In the real "real world," God's love is the operative reality. Thus, the poor in spirit are respected, those who mourn are comforted, the meek are honored, peacemakers are valued, and the persecuted are ministered to. To be sure, the old so-called "real world" has not literally, chronologically passed away; it and its values are perpetuated among those who continue to serve themselves rather than yielding themselves to God. But for those who yield themselves to God's claim, accepting the "invitation…to become citizens of a new Kingdom," there is a new world with a new and alternative set of values and priorities. As Paul put it, "if anyone is in Christ, there is a new creation" (2 Cor. 5:17)–a new world that becomes for them the real "real world."

It is this reality that is captured so well by REM's song "It's the End of the World As We Know It." We are not saying that this message is what REM intended to communicate. Their song makes no claim to be religious, and it can be construed in a variety of ways. For instance, it was used in the movie *Independence Day* in conjunction with an invasion of the earth by alien beings. Interestingly, however, the effect of the threat to the whole world was to unite traditional enemies in opposing the aliens. National, racial, and cultural barriers were overcome in the formation of a new world community. In this sense, the movie's depiction of "the end of the world as we know it" was not just the havoc created by the aliens but the new sense of unity and cooperation on a worldwide scale among former enemies. In this sense, the movie's depiction resembles Jesus' proclamation of the reign of God, into which Jesus invited *all people,* regardless of background, status, race, nationality, reputation, or merit. To be sure, this kind of worldwide, radically accepting, all-inclusive community does *not* characterize the so-called "real world" that we know so well. But it does characterize the reign of God, the real "real world," which, according to Jesus, makes the old world obsolete. As God's values and priorities are put into "visible, practical form" by those who accept Jesus' invitation, we witness "the end of the world as we know it." To participate in God's "new creation" is the essence of what Jesus calls "happy," "blessed," or "fortunate," a direction that REM moves with the phrase that follows "It's the end of the world as we know it"–namely, "and I feel fine."

Thus, REM's song, regardless of what message they may have intended, becomes a stimulus to think carefully, creatively, and faithfully about Jesus' proclamation of the end of the old, so-called "real world" and about his inauguration of "a new creation." We continue our thinking with the help of two songs by Tracy Chapman.

The Future Is Now

Jesus' proclamation of the reign of God as a present reality appears to be problematic on two counts:

1. If God rules the world, then why are there so many things wrong with human life and the world? In essence, this question poses the issue of theodicy, which we discussed in chapter 1. It is crucial to remember that God is essentially loving, and thus God chooses to exercise power as sheer love and not sheer force. In other words, God does not *force* people into submitting to God's rule, but rather *invites* people to enter God's reign. Because some people refuse the invitation, and because even those who accept the invitation are unable to put self-centeredness and self-assertion completely aside, God's intent for the world remains incomplete and the world remains broken. Thus, even when God's "new creation" takes "visible, practical form" among us, it is always in the midst of brokenness and incompletion. In this sense, God's people always live, as the Gospel of John suggests (see 17:15–19), *in* the world (that is, constantly in the midst of brokenness) but not *of* the world (that is, constantly experiencing amid brokenness the peace that derives from submitting the self to God's claim and surrendering self-assertion in favor of loving one another).

2. Given the brokenness of the world and the incompletion of God's intent for the world, what about those biblical passages that speak of the kingdom of God as a *future* reality? This question involves eschatology (literally, "a word about final things"), which we discussed in chapter 1 in relation to Joan Osborne's "One of Us." We suggested that not all parts of the New Testament look toward the cataclysmic end of the world at the time of the second coming of Christ. In particular, the Gospel of John anticipates no second

coming, because Jesus is *already here!* He is here, because he gave his spirit to his disciples, representing the church, on Easter evening (see Jn. 20:19–23). Thus, Jesus will not come again. For John, in other words, "the end of the world" has *already* happened! Jesus has inaugurated a new world, which John calls "eternal life." In essence, "eternal life" is John's term for what Matthew, Mark, and Luke call the "kingdom of God" or "the kingdom of heaven." In both cases, the so-called "real world" has ended, and a new creation has *already* begun.

What then do we say about those passages that anticipate a second coming? First, we simply acknowledge that the New Testament has preserved conflicting views. And in view of the fact that the apostle Paul, along with the authors of Matthew, Mark, and Luke, expected Jesus' second coming to occur *soon*, we can conclude that they were mistaken. In essence, John got it right! At the same time, those biblical passages that anticipate a second coming are not simply wrong or worthless. Rather, they preserve the helpful and truthful insight that because we sinful human beings can never completely set selfishness side, the experience of God's reign among us is never fully realized. In this sense, God's reign remains and will always remain the vision of a *future* reality toward which we live. And yet, amid our brokenness and incompletion, we really do know and experience the new creation that Jesus has inaugurated. In this sense, the future is *now!*

It's another paradox, a situation in which two seemingly contradictory conditions are both true (see chapter 2). When talking about the kingdom of God announced and embodied by Jesus, it's not a matter of either a present reality *or* a future reality. It is both! Two songs by Tracy Chapman help to communicate this paradox of "already" and "not yet." Her "Heaven's Here on Earth" even borrows from and paraphrases Mark 1:15 concerning the presence of the kingdom. The song concludes that "Heaven's Here on Earth" when people embody love in the service of peace. Although we could argue that Chapman has secularized Jesus' proclamation of the reign of God, since she doesn't mention God or

Jesus, she has nevertheless captured well the paradox of Jesus' teaching about the reign of God. "This *could be* heaven here on earth," she concludes (emphasis added). But as the title of the song has clearly suggested, sometimes already "Heaven's Here on Earth." But *not* everywhere and *not* always. We humans clearly do not always embody love in the service of peace. Thus, the reign of God does not always take "visible, practical form" among us; and we'll always have to conclude, as Chapman does, "This *could be* heaven here on earth."

The persistent reality of brokenness and incompletion is also communicated by Chapman in the song that immediately follows "Heaven's Here on Earth" on the CD titled *New Beginning.* The song is also titled "New Beginning," and its opening line suggests that the world is irretrievably broken. The rest of the song belies its initial pessimism, as it offers the invitation to make a new start and to do nothing short of "Create a new world." Especially when heard back to back, as they appear on the CD, Tracy Chapman's songs help us to grasp the paradox of Jesus' proclamation of the reign of God. It's not a matter of either/or, but of both/and. In Chapman's terms, "Heaven's Here on Earth," but a "New Beginning" is also invited that will change the world. In biblical terms, "the kingdom of God is at hand," but Jesus' invitation to "repent, and believe in the good news" is a perennial calling. Insofar as we respond, we do indeed change the world (see this book's Conclusion). The so-called "real world" comes to an end, and the *real* "real world" takes "visible, practical form" among us as God's "new creation." The future is now!

The Cradle and the Cross

The church has often so emphasized the saving significance of Jesus' death—the cross—that it has failed to appreciate the saving significance of Jesus' birth, life, and ministry. To be sure, Jesus' suffering and death reveal the depth of God's love for the world, but so does his life. As the Gospel of John suggests, the incarnation—Jesus' life in the flesh—already reveals God's "grace and truth." The affirmation echoes

Ex. 34:6, God's revelation of the divine self to Moses as "steadfast love and faithfulness." In short, Jesus's birth, life, and ministry reveal God's saving love just as surely as does Jesus' death.[2] The cradle and the cross belong together. Furthermore, the life Jesus lived between the cradle and the cross reveals the shape of the new creation–God's reign, the real "real world"–that Jesus announced.

As their titles suggest, the two songs discussed in this section begin with a focus on the cradle: Bruce Cockburn's "Cry of a Tiny Babe" and The Dave Matthews Band's "Christmas Song." But neither stops there. By retelling the Christmas story in Matthew 2, Cockburn communicates effectively that the cradle lies in the shadow of the cross. In "Christmas Song," The Dave Matthews Band moves explicitly to the crucifixion. Both Cockburn and The Dave Matthews Band also depict the shape of God's reign by describing the kind of people with whom Jesus associated. In so doing, both songs effectively communicate the scandalous nature of grace in the eyes of the so-called "real world," as well as the radical nature of a love that embraces all people. Jesus' embodiment of the reign of God evoked opposition in the first century A.D., and our acceptance of the invitation to embody God's reign will also evoke opposition today.

The first stanza of Cockburn's song is a poetic rehearsal of Mt. 1:18–23, the announcement of Jesus' birth to Joseph and Joseph's decision to entrust an unlikely future to God– including the birth of a son who isn't his! The second stanza is based on Matthew 2. Cockburn mentions the magi, but his emphasis is on Herod's attempt to kill Jesus, the function of which in the Gospel of Matthew is to anticipate the opposition to Jesus that culminated on the cross. The third stanza features those who did not oppose Jesus:

> There are others who know about this miracle birth:
> The humblest of people catch a glimpse of their
>   worth;
> For it isn't to the palace that the Christ child comes,
> But to shepherds and street people, hookers and bums

And the message is clear if you've got ears to hear
That forgiveness is given for your guilt and your fear
It's a Christmas gift you don't have to buy
There's a future shining in a baby's eyes.

The radical consequences of forgiveness and grace—the valuing of all people, including "The humblest"—are emphasized by the chorus, which occurs between stanzas and which concludes the song:

Like a stone on the surface of a still river,
Driving the ripples on forever,
Redemption rips through the surface of time
In the cry of a tiny baby

The image of a "redemption" that "rips through the surface of time" suggests the radicality of Jesus' message about the reign of God. In the first century A.D., Herod was threatened, but Jesus' message is still radical. It threatens entrenched power, which is based on privilege and justifies itself by appealing to merit ("We work hard," "We deserve the best," "We've earned it," etc.). Grace and forgiveness mean that everyone is acceptable to God—"street people, hookers and bums"![3] The *real* "real world" is indeed a new creation, anything but business, politics, and social propriety as usual.

The word for this gracious acceptance of all people as God's children is *love*. God is love! And in God's kingdom, love is the constituting reality. When this love takes "visible, practical form" among us, it means what William C. Placher calls "a community of equals and a community of grace."[4] The life of this community is focused upon the Lord's table, which Placher describes as follows:

At this meal, all are invited, never matter class or race or gender, and all come as equals, for Jesus is the host.[5]

In our merit-based, self-centered culture (see Mary Pipher's cultural analysis in chapters 1 and 2), Jesus' message of all-inclusive love will inevitably threaten the powers and structures that prevail. Undoubtedly, some persons will be threatened and resist the radical implications of forgiveness and grace. But some persons will have "ears to hear" and will accept Jesus' message as liberating, life-giving good news. As Cockburn recognizes, this "Christmas gift" that we "don't have to buy" creates a new world—"a future shining in a baby's eyes." In a real sense, as suggested above, this future is now in the presence of those who forsake self-assertion to submit themselves to God's claim. In short, God's future is now in the presence of love.

Our consideration of the shape of the community gathered by love anticipates the next chapter, but for now, it is important to note that *love* is the key word in "Christmas Song" by The Dave Matthews Band. In greeting Jesus, the wise men demonstrate love: "*love* is all around." As suggested above, the song moves from the cradle to the cross. The other repeated phrase in the song is this: "the blood of our children all around." The effect of the repetition is to articulate the opposition to Jesus. Precisely because he befriended people who were outcast and undesireable, Jesus was arrested, tried, and crucified. Although Jesus preached and embodied "*love*...all around," the effect of his ministry produced "blood...all around." Thus, the Lord's Supper, which the song also alludes to, is a celebration that recalls the inextricable connection between Jesus' love and Jesus' suffering and death.

"Christmas Song" eloquently communicates the inseparability of the cradle and the cross. The radical love that motivates God to enflesh Godself in the world is the same radical love that so threatens the so-called real world and its business, politics, and social propriety as usual. Insofar as North American culture encourages self-centeredness, greed, and exclusivity, to be a follower of Jesus will mean to be profoundly countercultural. Try welcoming into your home, neighborhood, or congregation "street people, hookers and bums," and see what your friends and neighbors think! There might even be organized opposition to your radical love. There certainly was organized opposition to Jesus' radical love, resulting in "the blood of our children all around." That is what Jesus meant when he said, "If any want to become my followers, let them deny themselves and take up their cross and follow me" (Mk. 8:34). To love as Jesus loved is to invite the same kind of opposition Jesus encountered. The radicality of Jesus' love is reinforced by two more songs about Jesus.

Party Time

Kevin Kinney's song, "Shindig with the Lord," is about Jesus' last supper with his disciples. Peter and Judas are mentioned, and the disciples are described as eating and drinking with Jesus as they look back over his life in preparation for his death. But the song looks beyond Jesus' suffering and death. Jesus points his disciples toward Easter, suggesting that it will be the point of his return. Because Jesus is back (see the earlier discussion of John's eschatology), the song becomes not just a song about the last supper, but also a song about *the Lord's supper*, the church's ongoing celebration of the presence of the living Christ. Actually, the opening line of the song has already anticipated this direction by mentioning not only Peter but also Paul, and suggesting further that Peter and Paul have arrived at the last supper from Arkansas. Of course, Paul was not at the Last Supper, and of course, neither Peter nor Paul came from Arkansas! This apparent discrepancy is the crucial clue that "Shindig with the Lord" is really about the *contemporary* celebration of the Lord's supper.

As such, Kinney's song clearly communicates the celebrative aspect of the Lord's supper, as well as the radical good news that all are invited to the table. As the title suggests, the Lord's supper is like a "Shindig with the Lord," a joyful party, and as Kinney extends the invitation, "Why don't you *all* come along" (emphasis added). To be sure, given the somber way most congregations observe the sacrament of the Lord's supper, most people don't think of it as a shindig or a party. But that's exactly what it's supposed to be. When we talk about *celebrating* the Lord's Supper, we should pay more attention to the word *celebrating!* Our liturgies say it, but we often miss the point that the Lord's Supper is "the *joyful feast* of the people of God." In short, it's party time! Or, as the title of Kinney's song suggests, it's a "Shindig with the Lord."

In this regard, Kinney's song is also a reminder of something that biblical scholars point out—namely, that we should see a real continuity between the Lord's supper and other instances in the gospels when Jesus *ate* with people. Eating is essentially a social activity, and it is crucial to notice that Jesus was willing to eat, and indeed did eat, with anybody and everybody![6] Jesus was radically inclusive, and it was precisely this radical inclusivity that caused some people to oppose him. In essence, Jesus was accused of partying too much and with the wrong people. As Jesus himself recognized, his opponents saw him as "'a glutton and a drunkard, a friend of tax collectors and sinners!'" (Mt. 11:19).

It is also crucial to notice that Jesus does not deny that his life and ministry are essentially a big party—not partying simply for the sake of partying, to be sure, but rather partying to celebrate that the old world has ended and the new creation has begun. In other words, Jesus' party celebrates the good news that God *loves* the world, and that God invites everybody into God's family. In one of the stories he told, Jesus even describes the reign of God as being like a "wedding banquet" (Mt. 22:2)—that is, a party or a shindig. And Jesus suggests that everybody is invited: "invite everyone you find to the wedding banquet" (Mt. 22:9).

Like "Cry of a Tiny Babe" and "Christmas Song," Kinney's song captures the radically inclusive nature of God's reign. All are invited to Christ's table: "Why don't you *all* come along" (emphasis added). At this point, the song recalls Placher's conclusion mentioned above: Because Jesus is the host, "all are invited" to the Lord's table. In the old world, the so-called "real world," social interaction is a means of separating, stratifying, excluding other people. That is to say, our parties usually include the people we like and the people who like us (or who are like us). But in the reign of God, the new creation, the *real* "real world," it is different. As Jesus told us and showed us, the old world is obsolete. It's party time! And when God throws a party, *everybody* is invited!

He's Back

The title of Collin Raye's song, "What If Jesus Comes Back Like That," makes it sound like the song is about the so-called second coming of Jesus. And in a sense, it is, but the way the song turns out actually suggests that Jesus is *already back* among us. The first stanza of the song describes a man whom others view as "a low down no account hobo." The first chorus then asks:

> What if Jesus comes back like that
> On an old freight train in a hobo hat
> Will we let him in or turn our back

The second stanza describes a crack baby, and the second chorus then asks:

> What if Jesus comes back like that
> Two months early and hooked on crack
> Will we let him in or turn our back

The third stanza, which the lyrics sheet describes as the "Bridge," shifts attention from the present to the past. It focuses on the cross, and then it reminds the listener how Jesus was born in humble circumstances:

> He came to town on a cold dark night
> A single star was his only light
> The baby born that silent night
> A manger for his bed

The recalling of Jesus' birth as a baby recalls the second stanza, and the phrase "He came to town," repeats the first line of the song when it was used of the hobo. The effect is to invite the listener to see Jesus in the faces of the "no account hobo" and the neglected child, thus recalling Mathew 25:40: "'Truly I tell you, just as you did it to one of the least of these who are members of my family, you did it to me.'" What this affirms is that God loves the whole world, and as Jesus demonstrated with his life and ministry, God claims "the humblest of people" as members of God's family, and

God invites us to do the same. Such is the shape of God's reign, God's new creation, the real "real world."

As for Jesus, what this means is that he's back! It's party time! The future is now! It's the end of the world as we know it!

NOTES

[1] Stanley Hauerwas and William H. Willimon, *Resident Aliens: Life in the Christian Colony* (Nashville: Abingdon Press, 1989), p. 87, italics added.

[2] For an articulate statement of this view and its implications, see Pamela Dickey Young, "Beyond Moral Influence to an Atoning Life," *Theology Today* (October 1995): 344–355.

[3] See Elsa Tamez, *The Amnesty of Grace: Justification by Faith from a Latin American Perspective* trans. Sharon H. Ringe (Nashville: Abingdon Press, 1993), especially pp. 129–140 (see chap. 1, note 16).

[4] William C. Placher, *Narratives of a Vulnerable God: Christ, Theology, and Scripture* (Louisville, Ky.: WJKP, 1994), p. 144.

[5] Ibid., p. 148.

[6] John Dominic Crossan captures well the pervasive and radical significance of this aspect of Jesus' life. See his *Jesus: A Revolutionary Biography* (San Francisco: Harper, 1994), pp. 45–48, 66–70.

FOUR

Facing the Music about the Church

All God's Children

It is understandable that one's view of the church follows from one's understanding of God and Jesus. In fact, chapter 3 has quite directly anticipated this chapter. Jesus' proclamation of the reign of God called a community into being. While at first this community consisted of a small core of disciples, it soon became the church. Known early on as "the body of Christ" (1 Cor. 12:27), the church consisted of those who, responding to Jesus' invitation to enter the reign of God (Mk. 1:15), attempted to give "visible, practical form" to what Jesus said and demonstrated about God.[1] It still does!

To be sure, theologians have always resisted a simple identification of the visible church with the reign of God— and with good reason, as we shall suggest below. But this raises the question: What constitutes the church? In the Reformation era, when this question was very much alive, John Calvin suggested that the church exists when and where the Word of God is "preached and heard and the sacraments administered according to Christ's institution."[2] The key words here are "heard" and "according to Christ's institution." When the Word of God is actually *heard,* people will be put in touch with the good news that God loves the whole world and that God is essentially gracious (see chapter 1). When the sacraments are *administered according to Christ's institution,* baptism is a celebration of God's gracious acceptance of all people; and the Lord's Supper is a meal hosted by Jesus, to which *everyone* is invited because *no one* deserves to be there. When the Word of God is preached and heard, and when the sacraments are administered according to Christ's institution, the result will be, in William Placher's words, "a community of equals and a community of grace."[3]

Placher continues by pointing out that the church will be marked by "inclusiveness":

> So should Christians always be indignant when what ought to be Jesus' church becomes a community of exclusion, celebrating in Robert Bellah's phrase, "the narcissism of similarity."
>
> Few issues illustrate so clearly the relation of liturgy [including the proclamation of the Word of God and the administration of the sacraments!] and Christian life as this question of inclusiveness...
>
> Just as the community of the baptized is one where one can be free to speak the truth and the community around the Lord's Table is one in which we share an equality so firm that different gifts can flourish, so a community that tells and truly hears the stories of the crucified Jesus will of necessity remain open to the outsiders and strangers of the world. A place

where the Word of God is preached and heard and
the sacraments properly administered makes for a
pretty good church.[4]

The songs in this chapter will help us explore what it
means to be the church, and inclusiveness will be a key
theme. We shall begin with three songs that help us to face
and acknowledge the many ways that the church throughout the centuries has failed to be faithful in communicating
God's Word and administering the sacraments according to
Christ's institution. The most direct and powerful in pointing out how the church has often been "a community of
exclusion" that celebrates "the narcissism of similarity" is
Todd Rundgren's song and video, "Fascist Christ." We'll then
move to Poison's "Something to Believe In" and Sting's "If I
Ever Lose My Faith in You."

The transition to more positive portrayals of what the
church is called to be will be made with a song titled "God
Help the Outcast." This song envisions inclusiveness on the
most expansive scale possible, suggesting quite biblically that
all people are children of God. Two additional songs, Prefab
Sprout's "One of the Broken" and Blind Melon's "No Rain,"
will help to fill out the implications of the affirmation that all
people are children of God.

Two additional songs conclude the chapter. Donna
Summer's "Forgive Me" highlights the reality that inclusiveness results fundamentally from grace and its inseparable
companion, forgiveness. James Taylor's "Shed a Little Light"
points again to the kind of worldwide inclusiveness that characterizes the church. By approaching this inclusiveness
through a celebration of Martin Luther King's vision, the
song touches upon the issue of racism and thus anticipates
chapter 5 and its consideration of the church's mission.

Utter Realism about the Church

In his book, *God and Ourselves: A Brief Exercise in Reformed
Theology*, Joseph D. Small suggests that "The Reformed
tradition provides us with two resources for faithful

discipleship: utter realism about the church and utter trust in the presence of the Holy Spirit."[5] The first three songs put us in touch with the first resource that Small mentions: "utter realism about the church."

A bumper sticker we saw recently reads as follows: "Jesus, Save Me from Your Followers!" The request eloquently articulates the fact that the church has often been and still often is "a community of exclusion." So does Todd Rundgren's song and video, "Fascist Christ." The title, of course, recalls the movement that earlier in this century allied with Nazism not only to exclude millions of people in the name of Christ, but to kill them as well—especially Jews, gypsies, and homosexuals. The computer-generated video effectively reinforces this horrible recollection as it depicts Roman crosses being twisted into swastikas, the symbol of Fascism and Nazism.

Rundgren is aware that the church has many sorry chapters in its history. He specifically mentions the Spanish Inquisition, but his real concern is that the horrors of the past are being threatened and repeated in the present. Rundgren is also aware of the good news that God loves the world and that all people are God's children. So, he aptly criticizes the

> strange philosophy in which God and man are enemies, in which there is no serenity unless you believe precisely what they want you to believe, and no diversity.

For there to be genuine inclusiveness, there must be diversity, or in Placher's terms, openness "to the outsiders and stranger of the world."

A lack of diversity will be nothing short of demonic. As Rundgren puts it: "The devil . . . rejoices when mankind has no choices, and power exploits us and peace avoids us." Again, inclusiveness is paramount, not for the sake of being "politically correct," but rather for sake of being faithful to the God who loves the whole world and who claims all people as God's children. Thus, Rundgren's song and video serve as a powerful statement of the indignation that Placher suggests should characterize Christians "when what ought to be Jesus' church becomes a community of exclusion."

Rundgren's message that the church often has and does serve demonic purposes rather than serving God's purposes is reminiscent of C. S. Lewis's *The Screwtape Letters*. In this book, a set of letters purporting to be from the devil, Screwtape, to one of his subordinates, Wormwood, Lewis also is utterly realistic about the church. For instance, after Wormwood has reported to his supervisor a setback for the forces of evil—one of his patients has become a Christian—Screwtape replies:

> One of our greatest allies at present is the Church itself. Do not misunderstand me. I do not mean the Church as we see her spread out through all time and space and rooted in eternity, terrible as any army with banners. That, I confess, is a spectacle which makes our boldest tempters uneasy. But fortunately it is quite invisible to these humans...When he [Wormwood's patient] gets to his pew and looks around him he sees just that selection of his neighbors whom he has hitherto avoided. You want to lean pretty heavily on those neighbors. Make his mind flit to and fro between an expression like "the body of Christ" and the actual faces in the next pew.[6]

In the way of utter realism, both Lewis and Rundgren agree that the church has often allied itself with the purposes of evil—hatred and exclusiveness—rather than the purposes of God—love that claims all the world as God's children.

Both Poison's "Something to Believe In" and Sting's "If I Ever Lose My Faith in You" focus our attention on the matter of faith or belief. In so doing, they also are utterly realistic about the church. For instance, the beginning of the video of "Something to Believe In" depicts a church, and the singer recalls being told to believe in Jesus as an image of televangelist Jim Bakker appears on a TV screen. But as the video unfolds, it becomes apparent that the kind of belief that the singer had encountered in church and from TV preachers is not sufficient for facing a world of evil, tragedy, and inequity. Three scenarios threaten his simplistic and unthinking faith. The first focuses on a Vietnam veteran who

is haunted by the horrors of the war in which he participated and who simply cannot make the readjustment to life
back home. The second scenario describes the death of a
best friend, and the third involves the singer's awareness of
homelessness in a land of plenty. As the final scenario concludes, the singer wonders why things are so bad for so many
people, and he, in essence, prays for "Something to Believe
In."

Each of the scenarios in the song has raised in its own
way the issue of theodicy, which we discussed in chapter 1.
Why war and its horrors? Why illness and untimely death?
Why rampant injustice? We need not rehearse that discussion here. Rather, the point here is that the church has often
been guilty of passing on a shallow and unthinking faith that
leaves people unprepared for the complex and ambiguous
realities of life. While Poison's song does not state this conclusion directly, it clearly implies it. For instance, take the
third scenario that involves the injustice of a situation in which
some people live in fabulous wealth while others are homeless. The church has often taught a doctrine of retribution
(again, see chapter 1) that suggests that the rich are wealthy
because God is rewarding them, and that the poor are suffering as a result of God's punishment. What this teaching
fails to realize is that the very rich are not generally wealthy
because they are good, but rather because they are ruthless
and selfish. Furthermore, this teaching cruelly blames the
poor for being poor, further victimizing those who are already victims. In contrast, to take seriously and to believe in
a God who loves the whole world and claims all people as
God's children would mean the awareness of "solidarity"
with and accountability to the poor.[7] In other words, it would
mean openness to outsiders and strangers, or, in short,
inclusiveness.

By failing to portray God properly (that is, failing to make
the Word of God *heard*), the church has left people in the
situation of crying out for "Something to Believe In." Poison's
song is an articulate example of caring and thinking persons
who are longing for a profound and meaningful interpretation of God and the world. As suggested in chapter 1 and

again here, this "Something" is the good news about a God who is essentially love, and thus who opens God's own self to vulnerability and suffering by choosing to be in genuine partnership with humankind in exercising dominion of the world.

Like Poison's "Something to Believe In," Sting's "If I Ever Lose My Faith in You" is an indictment of the church. Among the things that Sting suggests that he has lost faith in are science, progress, advertising, politics, and finally, the church. But Sting suggests that he has not, nor will he ever, lose faith in God. Addressing God in the song, he suggests that if he were ever to lose faith in God, "there'd be nothing left for me to do."

While Sting, Poison, and Todd Rundgren are utterly realistic about the church, their works are finally not only an indictment of the church, but also a challenge for the church to be faithful. Interestingly, neither Rundgren nor Poison nor Sting are utterly cynical. Rundgren implicitly commends a philosophy in which God and humans are partners rather than enemies; Poison suggests that there *is* "Something to Believe In"; and Sting very explicitly suggests this "something" is actually a someone–God. The interesting and crucial thing to notice is that these messages and conclusions are thoroughly biblical and that they are precisely what the church teaches and embodies when the Word of God is preached and heard and when the sacraments are administered according to Christ's institution. To be sure, the church has been and is unfaithful to God and God's purposes, and about this we must be utterly realistic. But at the same time, the church has preserved and transmitted the liberating and transforming good news of a God who loves the whole world and who claims all people as God's children; the church is still doing this sometimes and in some places.

In short, to use Small's words again, the church sometimes has and does display "utter trust in the presence of the Holy Spirit." When it does, it exists as "a community of equals and a community of grace." As such, it shuns the "narcissism of similarity"; and following from its trust in a God who loves the whole world, it practices a radical inclusiveness.

What this radical inclusiveness involves will be explored further with the help of several additional songs.

The Question of Inclusiveness

As we suggested above, citing William Placher, "this question of inclusiveness" is fundamental to the church's identity, not because inclusivity is "politically correct" but rather because it is *biblically correct.* This basic biblical message is clearly communicated by the song "God Help The Outcasts," two similar versions of which appear in the movie and on the soundtrack of Disney's *The Hunchback of Notre Dame.* The song is a prayer that is sung by the character Esmeralda, herself an outcast. But interestingly (and faithfully), she prays not for herself but for those who are even worse off than she. She concludes with what amounts to a statement of faith preceding a petition, affirming that all people are children of God and requesting what the title of the song suggests, "God Help the Outcasts."

As Esmeralda offers her humble prayer, other parishioners' voices can be heard in the background. They are praying for riches and recognition and power. But they have missed the point that *all* are the children of God. This affirmation pervades the Bible (see Gen. 12:1–3; Ps. 24:1), but Christians hear and see it most clearly in the life and ministry of Jesus, who, as John Dominic Crossan suggests, gathered around himself "a kingdom of nuisances and no-bodies"[8]–outcasts! Esmeralda's prayer hints at this even as it echoes a mistaken theology of retribution.

She suggests that because she is an outcast, she has no right to speak to God; but then it occurs to her to ask God if God too had not been an outcast. The question is right on target. If there's anything that Jesus' life and ministry affirms, it is that God took the form of an outcast–Jesus, the ridiculed, rejected, and eventually crucified one. Clearly, God was once an outcast! And just as clearly, this affirms God's love for the outcast. Jesus gathered around himself not the wealthy, the elite, the powerful, and the beautiful. Rather, he gathered around himself–that is, to say, he ate with or invited to his table–the poor, the humbled, the dispossessed, and the nobodies. What a lesson in inclusiveness! It was a lesson not lost on the apostle Paul, who affirmed that the cross reveals God's choice of the humble and the lowly to be God's own people (see 1 Cor. 1:18–31), a divine choice that shatters traditional social divisions among people (see Gal. 3:28). Furthermore, the cross reveals God's essential graciousness. In other words, *all people* belong to God because *no one* deserves it. And, as Elsa Tamez has pointed out (see above), it is precisely grace that means a fundamental "solidarity" among all people–or, in other words, inclusiveness. Indeed, according to the Bible, we all are the children of God!

What this means is demonstrated well by Prefab Sprout's song, "One of the Broken." The song makes specific references to two biblical characters, Moses and David, who communicated intimately with God. The issue for us, as the song frames it, is how appropriately to speak to, approach, or communicate with God. In the two stanzas of "One of the Broken," God is speaking and addresses this issue. What God wants is not singing that is addressed directly to God. Rather, God wants people to sing songs to "One of the Broken," as a way of honoring God. The message contained in "One of the Broken" echoes the words spoken by the Old Testament prophets on God's behalf. The prophetic speeches often open or conclude with the phrase, "Thus says the LORD," which Prefab Sprout paraphrases at the beginning of their song with the line, "Hi, this is God here." The prophets suggested that genuine worship consists not simply of ritual, music, and sacrifice, but rather of a proper relationship with God that is manifest in righteousness, justice, and love (see Isa. 1:12–18; Hos 6:6; Am. 5:21–24; Mic. 6:8). In biblical terms, justice and righteousness are always defined in terms of caring for and providing for the poor and needy (see Ps. 72:1–7, 12–14; 82:1–4). In other words, the issue again is inclusiveness. Proper worship or service to God consists in attentiveness to the broken. Everyone is to be included.

While this message derives from the prophets, it is clear that Jesus fulfills the prophetic tradition. Indeed, Jesus specifically says as much in Matthew 5:17. Furthermore, his words and deeds demonstrate that he attended to the broken. Prefab Sprout's "One of the Broken" is clearly reminiscent of Jesus' words in Matthew 25:40: "'Truly I tell you, just as you did it to one of the least of these who are members of my family, you did it to me.'" To serve the broken is to serve God. To include the broken is to commune with God. At the essence of God's will is openness "to the outsiders and strangers of the world."

While not as explicitly biblical and theological as "One of the Broken," Blind Melon's "No Rain" depicts the kind of inclusiveness that characterizes the faithful church. This message is especially clear when the words of the song are accompanied by the video. The plot of the video features the experience of an oddly dressed young woman (she is dressed like a bumblebee) who approaches several people on the streets of a city. She is apparently seeking a place in which to belong. As the words of the song express it, she wants a place where people will say to her, "I'll always be there when you wake." What the young woman seeks, however, is not a romantic relationship but a community. As the video unfolds, each encounter ends in rejection. Finally, the young woman wanders into the countryside where she sees an enclosure filled with people who are playing and dancing. There is a gate, but the gate is unlocked. When the young woman enters the gate, she is welcomed, accepted, and becomes part of the community. She belongs. She is included.

When the video of "No Rain" is viewed with the issue of the nature of the church in mind, then it stimulates people to ask, in effect, "Will the church be unlocked?" Will it keep people out, or will it invite people in? Almost every particular congregation will articulate the wish to grow. But often, there are strings attached, and other people are not really welcome unless they are "our kind of people." Will the church be open enough to affirm that all people are the children of God, even the outcast and the broken and the odd?

In other words, Blind Melon's "No Rain" helps us to sharpen our focus on "this question of inclusiveness." Especially when heard in conjunction with the more explicitly theological "God Help the Outcast" and "One of the Broken," this song reminds us that the when the Word of God is preached and heard and when the sacraments are administered according to Christ's institution, the church will be a place where everyone has a place. Shunning "the narcissism of similarity," the church will be open "to the outsiders and strangers of the world." It will be "a community of equals and a community of grace."

Compassion Happens

In focusing on the question of inclusiveness, we seem thus far to have emphasized equality more than grace. At this point, it is important to emphasize that equality and grace are inseparable realities in the Christian life. As we first mentioned in chapter 1, citing Elsa Tamez (see earlier in this chapter also), if we really believe in the grace of God, then we will live with a pervasive sense of gratitude and humility that will in turn result in what Tamez calls "solidarity" among all persons and classes of people. In other words, living by grace yields equality or inclusiveness, because no one thinks they are better or more deserving than anyone else.

The unfortunate reality is that while almost all church members would *say* they believe in grace, almost *no one* actually does! When it gets right down to it, most of us think we are pretty good people, who by our own hard work and ingenuity have *earned* what we have. If we believed in grace, then white people would not feel superior to black people, and rich or middle-class people would not look down on poor people. Furthermore, citizens of the United States would not blithely conclude that we *deserve* the lion's share of the earth's resources. In a nation that teaches self-sufficiency and the necessity to earn what we have, it is almost impossible to appreciate, much less embody, what it means to live by grace. This, of course, is precisely why the church, when it is faithful, is such a radical, countercultural, subversive institution–indeed, "a community of equals" *because* we are "a community of grace."

The relationship between grace and the compassion that leads to inclusiveness and equality is articulated beautifully in Donna Summer's "Forgive Me." Toward the beginning of the song, the words suggest that there are internal consequences when we pray, "Forgive me as I learn how to forgive." As the rest of the song makes clear, what happens inside when one is aware of being forgiven and attempts to embody forgiveness–that is, what happens when one lives by grace–is a life that is full of compassion, which means literally "suffering with." Compassion takes the form of blessing persons who persecute us, praying for our enemies, and showing mercy to them. In short, living by grace means the embrace of *all* other persons, even enemies, which is the ultimate in inclusiveness.

The line quoted above alludes, of course, to the Lord's Prayer: "Forgive us our debts as we forgive our debtors." And the song is actually a prayer addressed to Jesus, the one who from the cross prayed that his enemies be forgiven (see Lk. 23:34). The same radical inclusiveness that characterized Jesus' dying prayer also characterized his daily life and ministry, as he invited *all* to enter the reign of God and as he embodied compassion and inclusiveness by his willingness to eat with anyone and everyone. In other words, Jesus' formation of "a community of grace" meant the reality of "a community of equals." The two are inseparable. What *happens* when we pray for and embody forgiveness (that is, grace) is compassion that embraces all people, even our enemies (that is, equality).

Let Your Light Shine

Most people remember that Jesus said, "I am the light of the world" (Jn. 8:12). Fewer people remember that Jesus also said to his followers, "You are the light of the world . . . let your light shine before others, so that they may see your good works and give glory to your Father in heaven" (Mt. 5:14, 16). Jesus said this to his followers right after he had announced the presence of the reign of God (Mt. 4:17), and had declared "blessed" or "happy" the "poor in spirit," "those who mourn," "the meek," "those who hunger and thirst for righteousness," "the merciful," "the pure in heart," "the peacemakers," and "those who are persecuted for righteousness sake" (Mt. 5:3–10). These outcasts or broken ones are declared "happy" or "blessed" precisely because they are welcome in God's realm. They are children of God!

In this context, the "good works" that Jesus challenges his followers to do consist of living by grace and so creating a community in which all people are welcome, even and indeed especially the outcasts and the broken, or in Placher's terms, "the outsiders and strangers of the world." The final song discussed in this chapter, James Taylor's "Shed a Little Light," celebrates the kind of all-inclusive community that the church is called to be. It begins and ends by inviting listeners to contemplate Martin Luther King, Jr. and his message that people all over the world are bound together by a common humanity that includes "ties of hope and love." Taylor's words offer a beautiful description of what Elsa Tamez calls "solidarity," which she says results from the affirmation that we are saved by grace (see chapters 1 and 3, as well as earlier in this chapter). In other words, we all are children of God! To make this affirmation and to live by it is what Jesus means by letting our "light shine before others."

It is quite appropriate, therefore, that Taylor's song continues as a song about light. In accordance with the biblical affirmation that both Jesus and his followers are the light of the world, the song is both a prayer and a pledge. The title, "Shed a Little Light," becomes a request to God to illumine the world. But what the Lord is asked to do, the singers of the song also pledge to God to do–to "Shed a Little Light." When the prayer and the pledge are heard in the context of the opening and closing words of the song, it is clear that shedding light includes the gathering of a worldwide "community of equals and a community of grace."

Because the song also recognizes that our common humanity also involves the common task of gathering a worldwide community, it provides an appropriate transition to the next chapter. Chapter 5 will examine several songs that put us in touch with some of the specific tasks that contribute to the living out of the affirmation that all of us are children of God.

88 Facing the Music

NOTES

[1] Stanley Hauerwas and William H. Willimon, *Resident Aliens: Life in the Christian Colony* (Nashville: Abingdon Press, 1989), p. 87 (see above chap. 3, note 1).

[2] John Calvin, *Institutes of the Christian Religion*, ed. John T. McNeill, trans. Ford Lewis Battles (Philadelphia: Westminster Press, 1960), p. 1023 (4.1.9).

[3] William C. Placher, *Narratives of a Vulnerable God: Christ, Theology, and Scripture* (Louisville, Ky.: WJKP, 1994), p. 144 (see above chap. 3, note 4).

[4] Placher, *Narratives of a Vulnerable God,* p. 155.

[5] Joseph D. Small, *God and Ourselves: A Brief Exercise in Reformed Theology* (Louisville: Presbyterian Publishing, 1996), p. 40.

[6] C. S. Lewis, *The Screwtape Letters* (New York: MacMillan Publishing, 1961), p. 12.

[7] See Elsa Tamez, *The Amnesty of Grace: Justification by Faith From a Latin American Perspective,* trans. Sharon H. Ringe (Nashville: Abingdon Press, 1993), pp. 129-140 (see above chap. 1, note 16 and chap. 3, note 3).

[8] John Dominic Crossan, *Jesus: A Revolutionary Biography* (San Francisco: Harper, 1994), p. 54.

FIVE

Facing the Music about Mission

Sensitivity to All the Sufferings of Humanity

As chapter 3 anticipated chapter 4, so chapters 3 and 4 have anticipated this chapter. In other words, how one understands Jesus (chapter 3) and the nature of his "body," the church (chapter 4), affects how one understands the church's involvement in the world—its mission. This interrelatedness of Jesus, church, and mission is expressed well in the following section of the Presbyterian Church's "The Confession of 1967":

The life, death, resurrection, and promised coming
of Jesus Christ has set the pattern for the church's
mission. His life as [hu]man involves the church in
the common life of [all people]. His service to [hu-
manity] commits the church to work for every form
of human well-being. His suffering makes the church
sensitive to all the sufferings of [hu]mankind so that
it sees the face of Christ in the faces of [people] in
every kind of need. His crucifixion discloses to the
church God's judgment on [our] inhumanity to [one
another] and the awful consequences of its own complicity in injustice. In the power of the risen Christ
and the hope of his coming, the church sees the promise of God's renewal of [human] life in society and of
God's victory over all wrong.[1]

This statement of faith about Jesus, the church, and mission
highlights several crucial affirmations that lie at the heart of
this chapter and that build upon the affirmations made in
chapters 3 and 4.

First, "Jesus has set the pattern for the church's mission."
As suggested in chapter 3, Jesus' proclamation of the reign
of God meant "the end of the world as we know it" and the
beginning of "a new creation." This *real* "real world," as we
called it, reverses the values and priorities of the so-called
"real world." The operative reality is God's love, which Jesus
embodied and which becomes "the pattern" for the church's
life and the church's mission.

Second, Jesus' "life as [hu]man involves the church in
the common life of [all people]." As suggested in chapter 3,
Jesus' embodiment of God's love meant his openness to and
acceptance of *all people*. And as suggested in chapter 4, when
the church puts Christ's love into "visible, practical form," it
exists as "a community of equals and a community of grace."
In keeping with "the pattern" that Jesus set, the church shuns
"the narcissism of similarity" and is "open to the outsiders
and strangers of the world." In short, the church affirms that
all people are God's children, and so the mission of the church
involves "the common life of [all people]."

Third, because to be human means inevitably to suffer and to be needy (see chapter 2), the church's involvement with all people will mean that it will be "sensitive to all the sufferings of [hu]mankind" and attune to "every kind of need." Focusing on Van Halen's "Right Now" and The Graces's "Tomorrow," the first section of this chapter will identify various categories of suffering and need. Each of the following will be explored further in conversation with at least one song/video: racism (dc Talk, "Colored People"); poverty, including hunger and homelessness and one of their basic underlying causes, greed (Phil Collins, "Another Day in Paradise"; David LaMotte, "Butler Street"; Joni Mitchell, "Sex Kills"; Sweet Honey in the Rock, "Are My Hands Clean?"); HIV/AIDS (Elton John, "The Last Song"); and war/violence (Judy Collins, "Song for Sarejevo").

Fourth, an examination of the sufferings and needs of humankind inevitably calls attention to the issue of justice. As suggested in chapter 4, the prophets called for justice and righteousness, and they defined justice and righteousness as caring for and providing for the poor and needy. Jesus' fulfillment of the prophetic tradition means that justice is a crucial piece of "the pattern" that Jesus has set for the church's mission. Several of the songs mentioned above will call attention to justice, as well as invite us to consider our "own complicity in injustice."

Fifth, despite the discouraging persistence of injustice in the forms of racism, poverty, hatred, and violence, the church is empowered by the risen Christ to see signs of hope and "the promise of God's renewal of [human] life in society and of God's victory over all wrong." Tracy Chapman's "Why?" will remind us that this promise does not dilute our accountability. At the same time, however, it is hope that provides us strength and vision for the ongoing struggle, as suggested by Garth Brooks's "We Shall Be Free."

Right Now

When Jesus proclaimed the reign of God, he said "The time is fulfilled, and the kingdom of God is at hand; repent, and believe in the good news" (Mk. 1:15). In other words, *right now* is the time. To be sure, as we suggested in chapter 3, there is a sense in which the reign of God always remains a future reality as well. But it does not remain a future reality at the expense of its presence *now*—thus, the conclusion in chapter 3 that "the future is now." There is an urgency to Jesus' announcement of and his invitation to enter the reign of God.

This sense of urgency is captured well by Van Halen's song and video, "Right Now." The lyrics begin as follows:

> Don't wanna wait 'til tomorrow.
> Why put it off another day?
> One by one cruel problems
> build up and stand in our way ....
> Come on, turn, turn this thing around, right now;
> Hey, it's your tomorrow, right now;
> It means everything.

As the lyrics communicate the sense of urgency, the video provides graphics that reinforce the message by way of the pervasive repetition of "Right Now." One of the graphics even recalls Mk. 1:15 as it announces, "Right Now Is a Good Time to Repent." Repent literally means "to turn around," so the language of repentance also informs the lyrics of the song (see above).

The graphics also invite attention to what "The Confession of 1967" called "the sufferings of [hu]mankind" and "every kind of need." For instance, early in the video, the following appears: "Right Now Justice Is Being Perverted in a Court of Law." Not only does this reminder specifically recall the prophets (see Am. 5:7, 10, where "gate" refers to the court system), but it also serves to raise the crucial issue of justice. Like the prophets also, the effect is to invite us to consider our "own complicity in injustice."

Subsequent graphics have the same effect. It is not necessary to mention them all. Rather, we shall highlight several of the graphics that identify areas of suffering and need that set the agenda for the rest of the chapter. For instance, the following graphic introduces the issue of racism and invites attention to its causes: "Right Now Blacks and Whites

Don't Eat Together Very Much." Since, in the Christian tradition, eating together is a fundamentally important activity (see chapters 3 and 4), this graphic invites consideration of the Christian mission to welcome all people to the Lord's Table and consideration of our failure to do so—the church's "own complicity in injustice."

Other graphics introduce realities that are involved in creating and perpetuating poverty: "Right Now Oil Companies and Old Men Are in Control," as well as "Right Now Someone Is Working Too Hard for Minimum Wage." While no graphic explicitly mentions HIV/AIDS, one of them focuses on an issue that is relevant to a consideration of the suffering involved: "Right Now No One Is Safe From Loneliness." As for the suffering caused by war and violence, the following graphics are relevant: "Right Now There's a Bomb Factory Hard at Work," and "Right Now Our Government Is Doing Things We Think Only Other Countries Do." The effect of each of these graphics is to invite sensitivity to "the sufferings of [hu]mankind" and consideration of our "own complicity in injustice," both of which are fundamental to the church's mission.

The further effect, as suggested above, is to communicate the urgency of the sufferings and need afflicting us and all humanity. This effect is reinforced by another song, "Tomorrow," by The Graces. "Right Now" begins with the line, "Don't wanna wait 'til tomorrow," and it later offers the challenge, "It's your tomorrow." The Graces issue an identical challenge. The first verse of the song describes the plight of a homeless woman who is left to spend the night in a cold alley. The final line of the verse suggests to the listener that he or she might be able to assist this person tomorrow. The second verse describes a lonely, neglected man. It too concludes with the suggestion to the listener that he or she might be able to help this person tomorrow. The final verse solidifies the point. It calls our attention to the fact that all too often we let tomorrow pass without doing anything, and it concludes with the invitation: "Don't wait until tomorrow."

That is the challenge as the church considers its mission in light of "the sufferings of [hu]mankind" and "every kind of need": "Don't wait until tomorrow." Or, as Jesus put it, "the kingdom of God is at hand; repent, and believe in the good news" (Mk. 1:15). Right now!

Racism

One of the most pervasive sources of "the sufferings of humanity" is racism. The history of the United States of America is a tragic story. The Native American population was decimated by settlers from Europe, and the institution of slavery victimized Africans for hundreds of years. The destructive effects are still with us, and racism itself remains an ugly reality of American life. As "Right Now" reminds us, "Right Now Blacks and Whites Don't Eat Together Very Much." As suggested earlier, this fact should be of particular concern to us Christians, since the centerpiece of our worship is the table of the Lord, a table at which all people are welcome to eat.

The church's mission in the midst of ongoing racism is to follow "the pattern" that Jesus set when he willingly ate with all people (see chapter 3). When we fail to do so, the results are tragic and far reaching. As William Placher points out, the beginning of apartheid in South Africa was the decision by the Dutch Reformed Church to conduct separate communion services for different races.[2] The history of the church's response to racism in the United States is just as tragic, and the unfortunate reality is that the Sunday morning worship hour is the most segregated hour of the week.

The song "Colored People" by dc Talk invites us to consider the history and reality of racism, our "own complicity in injustice," and the call to recognize our common humanity. The point is that the skin of people of all races is "colored," and that these "diverse tones" are a "thing of beauty" that represents "God's design." The song invites consideration of the history and reality of racism with the lines "we live in a tainted place" and "We've got a history so full of mistakes." By reminding us of our "own complicity in injustice," however, dc Talk intends not to condemn but rather to call us to repentance (see Mk. 1:15): "Repentance is the cure."

The song also depicts what repentance will mean:

We gotta come together, and thank the maker of us all…
We are colored people who depend on a Holy Grace…
We gotta come together, aren't we human after all?

The church's mission in the face of pervasive and persistent racism is to proclaim the good news that indeed God is "the maker of us all." In other words, *all people* are God's children (see chapter 4). As dc Talk recognizes, the appropriate response to "Holy Grace" is gratitude ("thank the maker of us all"). And, as we have suggested previously with reference to Elsa Tamez, to live by grace and gratitude results in "solidarity," because no one will conclude that they are better or more deserving than anyone else.[3] In other words, only the recognition that "we depend on a Holy Grace" will allow us to "come together," acknowledging our common humanity because we acknowledge that all are children of God. To proclaim and embody this good news is at the heart of the church's mission.

Poverty: Hunger, Homelessness, and Greed

As we saw in chapter 4, Poison's "Something to Believe In" highlighted the reality of poverty—homelessness and hunger—in a land of plenty. Their question of why things are so bad for so many people led to the prayerful request , "Give me something to believe in." The way Poison confronts the issue of poverty could imply that the problem is *God's* fault. But as we pointed out in the previous chapter, the rich are wealthy and the poor are needy *not* because God wants it to be that way, but rather because some people ruthlessly and greedily claim more than their share of our nation's and the earth's resources. In other words, the problem of poverty is *our* fault, and it invites us to consider our "own complicity in injustice."

As Mary Pipher points out, the problem of poverty is not just *their* problem; it is *our* problem, *everyone's* problem. She also suggests quite clearly that the real issue is the greed that our economic system encourages:

Our land of opportunity has become a land of opportunists. Our most organized religion is capitalism, which at its meanest turns virtue upside down. Predators become heroes, selfishness is smart and compassion is softheaded. Capitalism favors what's called the survival of the fittest, but really it's survival of the greediest, most driven and most ruthless. We have cared more about selling things to our neighbors than we've cared for our neighbors. The deck is stacked all wrong and ultimately we will all lose.[4]

In our experience, it is very difficult to get people, especially relatively prosperous North Americans, to think about the problem of poverty as *everyone's* problem and even as *everyone's* fault. In other words, it is difficult for us to claim "solidarity" with all other people, because we are taught to think and act individualistically. There is a song by Sweet Honey in the Rock that may begin to help people appreciate what it means to think other than individualistically. The song is titled "Are My Hands Clean?" And quite appropriately, in light of Mary Pipher's analysis, it is a song about buying and selling. In particular, the song invites us to consider our "own complicity in injustice" as it points out how much it costs *other people* when we buy something at a discount price in a North American department store.

The song opens with the acknowledgement that the clothes we wear are made by people in other countries. The song then traces in detail the process involved in the manufacturing of a cotton-polyester blouse that can be purchased inexpensively by North American women at a department store. As the lyrics point out, the story begins in Central America, where workers picking cotton make $2.00 a day. The cotton is then shipped to the southern United States by way of the Panama Canal. Meanwhile, the synthetic component (polyester) is manufactured in the United States from oil from South America, where the workers in the oil fields make $6.00 a day. The polyester fibers are then shipped overseas to be upgraded. The cotton and polyester fibers end up again in the United States, where they are woven into fabric, which then returns to the Third World. In Haiti, women work for $3.00 a day to sew the fabric into blouses. The blouse is shipped to the United States, where it can then be purchased inexpensively, especially during a discount sale. The title of the song forms the question that concludes the song. It is posed by ones in the privileged position to buy the blouse: "Are My Hands Clean?"[5]

Clearly, Sweet and Honey in the Rock suggest that the answer to this question is *no*. What their song involves is called *full-cost pricing*. In other words, they recognize that *someone* is paying dearly for the blouse, but it is *not* the consumer in the United States. Rather, it is the cotton-pickers in El Salvador, the oil workers in Venezuela, and the piece workers in Haiti. People in other nations are paying dearly for what people in the United States can buy for next to nothing. In short, we are living at the expense of others. This is our "own complicity in injustice." Unfortunately, the production and marketing of cotton-polyester blouses is not an isolated example. The same situation exists for items like coffee, bananas, gasoline, athletic shoes, and a host of others. As Mary Pipher suggests, our economic system encourages and rewards greed. We care more about buying and selling than we do about each other.

While "Are My Hands Clean?" makes clear the detrimental effects of our greed on God's children in other countries, Joni Mitchell's "Sex Kills" suggests how our greed also hurts our own selves; in Mary Pipher's words, we are all losing. Very appropriately, Mitchell begins her song with a focus on justice. She sees a license plate on a car that reads "JUST ICE," and she wonders if justice has become "just ice," something that is quickly melting away before our eyes.

> Is Justice just ice?
> Governed by greed and lust?
> Just the strong doing what they can
> And the weak suffering what they must?
> And the gas leaks,
> And the oil spills,

> And sex sells everything,
> And sex kills...
> Sex Kills.

In essence, Mitchell suggests that our national tradition of "justice for all" has given way to greed and its destructive, indeed deadly, effects. The strong take advantage of the weak, and as is inevitable in a situation in which greed rules, selling is paramount. Even sex, which should be an intimate form of unity among human beings, has become a means that is used by advertisers to sell their products—"sex sells everything."

Mitchell does not intend to say that sex itself is bad or harmful. Rather, Mitchell suggests that in a situation in which sex has been co-opted by greed, the results will be devastating and deadly. In this sense—that is, in *our* contemporary context—"sex kills." The lyrics quoted above suggest that one of the deadly effects of our greed is environmental pollution—"the gas leaks" and "the oil spills." Later in the song, she mentions further environmental damage and its human toll:

> The ulcerated ozone
> These tumors of the skin—
> This hostile sun beatin' down on
> This massive mess we're in!

The depletion of the ozone layer is potentially catastrophic and deadly, and we are already experiencing the early effects—alarmingly increased rates of skin cancer and global warming, which produces further effects such as the El Niño phenomenon that played havoc with the weather in the United States during the fall of 1997 and the winter and spring of 1998.

Mitchell's concern about how our greed has affected the environment, and how the environment is in turn affecting us, calls to mind again the importance of full-cost pricing. In the United States, businesses and industries have been allowed and still are being allowed in many instances to operate *without the cost* of cleaning up the pollution that they generate. The motive, of course, is greed (although we often call it something like "progress" or "economic growth"). In other words, the owners of the businesses and industries can make more money when they don't have to be responsible for the future of the environment, and we consumers can pay less for what the industries produce and the businesses sell. But, from the perspective of full-cost pricing, we realize that *someone* is paying dearly for the neglect of the environment. In fact, *we* are! *All of us* are paying for the greed that leads to the pollution and destruction of the environment. The people who get skin cancer–not to mention the increased rates of other cancers that can probably be linked to chemicals in the environment–are literally paying with their lives, and everyone is paying in terms of increased medical costs. *All* of us pay too for the destructive and often deadly effects of floods and severe weather produced by global warming. Again, some people pay with their lives, but everyone must pay in the form of disaster relief, higher insurance rates, and the haunting anxiety that we may be slowly destroying the very earth that sustains our lives. Insofar as *we* are not paying now for our greed, then future generations will certainly have to bear the cost of our greed and its destructive effects. When "sex sells everything," then "sex kills."

Mitchell recognizes the deadly effects of greed not only in the environmental arena but also in the realm of human relatedness, or the lack thereof. Our society's focus on buying and selling teaches us to value *things* above all, and it teaches us to measure our happiness in terms of whether we get what we want. In short, our economic system encourages and rewards ruthless self-centeredness and greed. Obviously, self-centeredness and greed do not contribute to the inclusiveness and "solidarity" that God wills for human communities and that follow from the affirmation that *all* people are children of God (see chapters 3 and 4). Instead, as Mitchell suggests, self-centeredness and greed lead to unforeseen and unfortunate results. Instead of the happiness that we expect from buying things, we experience worrisome and debilitating debt ("the bills bury you like an avalanche"). Instead of the harmony that would result from caring for one another, our self-centeredness produces a sense of entitlement that puts us at each other's throats ("And lawyers haven't been this popular/Since Robespierre slaughtered half of France!"). Not surprisingly, our conflicted society yields excessive violence ("Oh and the tragedies in the nurseries–/Little kids packin' guns to school"). And Mitchell also picks up on the "road rage" that has become a sort of symbol for our times:

> You can feel it out in traffic;
> Everyone hates everyone!

This is precisely what Mary Pipher meant when she suggested that, on account of our selfishness and greed, "ultimately we will all lose." Indeed, Joni Mitchell's song can be thought of as a poetic, musical rendering of Mary Pipher's assessment of contemporary culture. When what is supposed to communicate human intimacy and caring is put in the service of greed, then we shall all lose. When "sex sells everything," then "sex kills."

Indeed, as Joni Mitchell suggests, we *all* are already losing. The pollution and destruction of our environment, the epidemic of rage, the daily violence that we have learned to take for granted, the replacement of caring for one another by hatred for another–all these realities describe the "massive mess we're in!" These realities affect us all, and they are part of *the full cost* we all are paying for structuring a society in which buying and selling are paramount. They indicate, in other words, our "own complicity in injustice."

While *all* of us and our quality of life suffer as a result of the "massive mess" we find ourselves in, there are certain people who are particularly victimized. Two more songs invite our consideration of the plight of the poor, as well as the daily realities of existence for many of the poor–homelessness and hunger. The first song is "Another Day in Paradise" by Phil Collins, and it is especially effective when heard while viewing the video. The video begins and ends with a view of the planet earth from space, suggesting the theological view that we have articulated throughout this book–namely, that because God claims the whole world and all its people, we are all in this *together*. The beginning and end of the video are the only parts that are in color.

The lack of color throughout the video symbolizes the stark reality that we simply do not acknowledge our togetherness or "solidarity" as children of God. In other words, we fail to care for and provide for each other. Therefore, what is, in one sense, "another day for you and me in paradise," is a much better day for some people than for others. The lyrics focus on the situation of a homeless woman:

> She calls out to the man on the street:
> "Sir, can you help me?
> It's cold and I've nowhere to sleep.
> Is there somewhere you can tell me?"
> He walks on, doesn't look back.
> He pretends he can't hear her,
> starts to whistle as he crosses the street.
> She's embarrassed to be there.
> Oh, think twice,
> 'cause it's another day for you and me in paradise...
> Think about it.

Collins's use of the word "think" is effective. He challenges us to "Think about it"—that is, to think about things we'd rather ignore. Like the man in the lyrics, we'd rather ignore the hungry and the homeless. We'd rather pretend not to hear; we'd rather turn our backs and walk away, whistling to cover up our "own complicity in injustice."

The song and video together also remind us effectively of the scope of the problem of poverty. While the lyrics focus on a specific woman, the video pictures hundreds of hungry and homeless women, men, and children as they sleep on streets and sidewalks and as they beg for food. Graphics document the stark statistics:

> One Billion People Have Inadequate Shelter
> 3 Million Homeless in America
> 100 Million Homeless Worldwide

Then, too, there's the billboard that, like our system as a whole, encourages greed rather than generosity:

> Please Don't Give To Beggars
> They Cause Traffic Problems

We'd much rather think that poor people are an inconvenience we can ignore rather than a sign of our "own complicity in injustice."

As Collins finally reminds us, the problem of poverty is not just a sociological one but rather a theological one. The song becomes a prayer:

> O Lord, is there nothing more anybody can do?
> O Lord, there must be something you can say.

As we have suggested previously, there is something God says! God says that *all* people are God's children. God says that God wants the church to be "open to the outsiders and strangers of the world." God says, through Jesus Christ, that those who minister to the least of their sisters and brothers are ministering to Christ himself (Mt. 25:31–40). To address Collins' question, God says that there is more that *all* of us can do. Indeed, this "more" is the church's mission for which Jesus Christ "has set the pattern."

David LaMotte's song titled "Butler Street" explicitly brings Jesus Christ into the consideration of the issue of poverty and greed in a way that reinforces the directions in which we have pointed throughout this book. The first two stanzas of the song are a critique of a completely individualistic outlook that says "nothing of love." Then the chorus articulates the logical results of this kind of view:

> Sing me a song about Jesus
> But please don't sing about the poor
> It's already been a long day
> I really don't want to hear anymore
> Sing me a song about Jesus
> That will make me feel happy inside
> Sing me a song about forgiveness
> That will make this lifestyle feel justified
> Sing a song about Jesus.

As we have suggested previously, all too often North American Christians have preferred to think about and talk about their faith solely in individualistic terms. As LaMotte points out, however, what this inevitably amounts to is an attempt to make ourselves feel good and right. In other words, it is an exercise in self-justification that allows us to ignore completely our "own complicity in injustice." Then too, of course, we miss completely the "solidarity" that God wills among human beings and that comes from openness "to all the sufferings of [hu]mankind" and from the sensitivity to see "the face of Christ in the faces of [people] in every kind of need."

In keeping with this kind of sensitivity, LaMotte sees the face of Christ in the faces of the poor that he runs into on Butler Street, a street in Atlanta, Georgia, where the Open Door Community serves breakfast daily to the homeless. As he puts it:

> Ran into Jesus this morning
> He was down on Butler Street
> He was carrying his bedroll
> He was standing in line for something to eat
> He got splashed by the muddy water
> When the shiny hubcaps rolled by
> He brushed himself off and chuckled and looked
>   over at me
> And said, "Hey, there but for the grace
>   of God go I."

Notice the difference between the kind of faith that LaMotte articulates and the individualistic stance that typifies much of North American Christianity. LaMotte's faith does not blame the poor for being poor, thus further victimizing those who are already victims. Rather, LaMotte values the poor as persons in whom the face of Christ can be seen.

Caution is in order at this point. LaMotte does not romanticize poverty in a manner that would allow the prosperous to avoid consideration of their own lifestyles and "complicity in injustice." In a striking reversal, however,

LaMotte's poor Jesus utters the saying that rich people usually utter when confronted with the poor: "There but for the grace of God go I." When rich people say this, the implication is that God has rewarded them and that God's grace has *not* extended to others. But when poor people say this, the implication is that God's grace extends to them as well. As we pointed out in chapters 3 and 4, Jesus and his ministry "set the pattern" for this understanding of grace.

Liberation theologians sometimes call this understanding of grace "God's preferential option for the poor." But this label can be misleading. It's not that God loves poor people more than rich people, but rather that poor people are in a better position *to prefer God* simply because they lack the *self-sufficiency* of the prosperous and the powerful. Thus, it would be more accurate perhaps to speak of "the poor's preferential option for God." But of course, this too can be misleading, because poverty itself certainly does not guarantee faithfulness.

In any case, LaMotte's "Butler Street" articulates the kind of faithfulness that Jesus himself talked about and embodied in a ministry that welcomed the stranger and the outcast. It is this kind of piety–one that detects the dignity of all persons as children of God and results in "solidarity" among people–that forms "the pattern for the church's mission." The homeless and hungry are not to be ignored but rather sought out, welcomed, and valued. This pattern may take a variety of forms–building homes through Habitat for Humanity and similar programs, soup kitchens, food pantries, clothes closets, homeless shelters and programs like Room at the Inn (where homeless persons are invited to spend the night in church buildings), lobbying for legislation that will not penalize the poor nor further victimize them, educational efforts aimed to counter the greediness fostered by our economic system, and more–but all these forms will communicate the church's mission "to work for every form of human well-being."

HIV/AIDS

One of the most publicized forms of human suffering in recent years is the outbreak and spread of HIV and the disease it causes, Acquired Immune Deficiency Syndrome (AIDS). While many within the church and our society have responded with concern and compassion, many others have not, and so AIDS has become a source not only of physical suffering but also a source of intense emotional suffering in the form of guilt, loneliness, and alienation. Some families have refused to see or even acknowledge the existence of their children who have AIDS. The disease itself is often only part of the issue; the other aspect is the fact that AIDS has higher rates of occurrence among gay men.

The church family has often responded as poorly to its children as have individual biological families. As is the case with poverty, the doctrine of retribution has often been invoked to blame the victims for their suffering. Some Christians even suggest that AIDS represents God's punishment on homosexuality, despite the fact the AIDS is not and never has been limited to the gay/lesbian community. Of course, blaming of the victim has then led to the further conclusion that they are to be condemned, shunned, and isolated.

It has been rightly suggested that AIDS in our time represents what the disease of leprosy represented in the time of Jesus. Lepers were viewed as unworthy and unclean, an abomination to God, and a threat to the health and well-being of the larger community. They were condemned, shunned, and isolated. But *not* by Jesus! Jesus touched them (see Mt. 8:4) and visited in their homes (Mt. 26:6–13), a sign of acceptance and "solidarity," or in short, love.

Jesus' pattern of behavior toward lepers points the way for the contemporary church in responding to AIDS–love that leads to "solidarity" rather than condemnation that leads to isolation. This way is articulated movingly in Elton John's, "The Last Song." The lyrics are sung from the perspective of a young man who is dying from AIDS. They indicate his pain, his anger, his fear, and his need to be accepted by and reconciled with those around him. The video, which Elton John produced to address the misunderstanding and bigotry that surrounds the issue of AIDS, adds a great deal to the words as it depicts effectively the young man's pained isolation. He cries out for someone to embrace him, and he confesses his need for a human touch to help him stay calm. As the song and video unfold, it becomes clear that he is talking to his father, who comes to take his son's hand and to embrace him in a hug of loving acceptance. The son's response poignantly reveals the loneliness and isolation that AIDS so often represents, as he celebrates incredulously the fact that his father comes to him and loves him. The father's loving touch of acceptance is healing. It does not produce a physical cure for the disease, but it is healing nonetheless. In the son's words, "That kind of understanding sets me free."

The liberating touch of love is what represents healing or salvation (our English word "salvation" is derived from a Latin word that means "to heal"; see the English word "salve," which means an ointment that assists physical healing). It is, as suggested above, the liberating touch of love that characterizes Jesus' response to leprosy, and Jesus "has set the pattern for the church's mission" in response to AIDS. We cannot effect a physical cure (although we may contribute financially and otherwise to the search for one), but we can offer the healing touch of love that leads to acceptance rather than rejection, to reconciliation rather than isolation, and to liberation rather than condemnation.

War

Throughout human history, one of the leading causes of "the sufferings of [hu]mankind" has been war. Jesus himself was a victim of human military prowess, and countless millions of people before and since Jesus' time have suffered at the violent hands of military strategists and soldiers. Given the glorification of war and violence in history books, in movies (both action films and documentaries), on television, and now in contemporary advertisements ("We Need a Few Good Men," "Be All That You Can Be," etc.), it is important that Christians at least attempt to think about war theologically.

A first step in this process is not to glorify war but rather to attempt to understand it for the horror that it is. Judy Collins's "Song for Sarejevo" can help. Collins wrote the song to honor the children of what used to be Yugoslavia, as

well as to remind the world of the sufferings of these children. The song is written from the perspective of a child in
Sarejevo, a once thriving city that has now been almost completely destroyed by the violence in Bosnia-Herzogovina.
The child recalls once having had a home and a normal life,
but all that is gone, and she has no one to protect her. The
song turns to a reflection on the war in Bosnia-Herzogovina,
but the words apply across the centuries, because they suggest that war dashes children's dreams and hopes for any
decent future. In the midst of war, the child in the song
dreams of peace, and she asks the adults of the world some
pointed and poignant questions about why they cannot stop
the wars that kill people and rob children of their childhoods,
if not their very lives. Her question, in essence, is this: Why
can't I live in the kind of world "where I can be a child?"

To be sure, force may sometimes be necessary to oppose oppressors. In a real sense, the military presence of the
United States and other nations stopped the war in Bosnia-
Herzogovina, and the continued presence of the armed forces
of the United States and the United Nations is maintaining a
semblance of peace in the region. But all too often, even in
the history of the United States, armed force has been used
to further self-centered economic and political agendas (consider, for instance, Vietnam, Panama, Grenada, etc.).

This reality, as well as an acute awareness of the horror
of war, invite us to think theologically about war. As ethicist
Stanley Hauerwas frequently points out in public speeches,
significant progress toward world peace would be achieved
*if just the Christians in the world would agree to stop killing other
Christians!* Or, to put it in explicitly theological terms, God
is always the loser in every war, because it is inevitably God's
children who are killed. This is the case because God claims
the whole world and all its peoples (see Ps. 24:1).

In other words, God always wills peace. When God's
claim on the world is announced in the Bible, the essence of
God's will is stated in terms of justice and righteousness (see
Ps. 96:13; 97:2; 98:9; 99:4); and justice and righteous produce *shalom*, "peace" (Ps 72:7). God's will for the world is
harmony among all peoples, all nations, and indeed, all

creation (see Isa. 2:1–4; 11:1–10; Mic 4:1–4). In rare instances, violent force may be necessary to oppose oppressors and their violence; however, God's will is ultimately
shalom. It is revealing that Jesus met institutionalized violence with sacrificial love. It is the church's mission to
follow Jesus' pattern. If force is ever to be used, the church
will insist that it be used not to protect the economic advantages of the United States or any other nation, but
rather to combat oppressors who would threaten the lives
or well-being of any of God's children.

"We're All Free" Or "We Shall Be Free": What Is Freedom?

Two final songs call further attention to the sufferings
and needs of humanity that have been in view throughout this chapter—poverty (and the greed that causes it),
loneliness, racism, environmental distress, and violence
and war. Furthermore, Tracy Chapman's "Why?" and
Garth Brooks's "We Shall Be Free" have one more thing
in common. They both feature the word "free," and the
contrasting senses in which they use the word "free" highlight a major dilemma in appropriating the Gospel in
North America. Namely, as Tracy Chapman suggests,
North Americans generally think that to be "free" means
to do and to pursue without restriction whatever we want
as individuals. On the other hand, Garth Brooks suggests
that to be "free" is something very different. It is a *corpo-
rate, communal* experience, and it means nothing short of
the elimination of hunger, homelessness, racism, prejudice, environmental pollution, greed, and alienation.

As Chapman further suggests, to be "free" in the sense
of doing whatever we want to do is disastrous. She begins
with a series of questions about "Why?" there is hunger,
alienation, war, and violence against women in a world where
there is plenty of food, people, and resources.

She then proposes an answer to these questions that
sounds much like Joni Mitchell's description of the "mess
we're in" (see earlier discussion). We are beset with problems like hunger, loneliness, war, and violence because we

think "we're all free" to do whatever we want to do as individuals.

Chapman quite helpfully, and quite accurately from a biblical perspective, suggests that this kind of freedom is illusory. Our so-called freedom is costing us dearly, and someday we'll all have to pay (see earlier discussion on full-cost pricing), as the conclusion to "Why" clearly suggests. Chapman's conclusion to "Why?" is her version of Mary Pipher's warning: "The deck is stacked all wrong and ultimately we will all lose." But, as we have suggested, and as Tracy Chapman suggests too, we all are *already* losing.

This is exactly what Garth Brooks affirms in "We Shall Be Free." In other words, Brooks suggests that we will not *really be free* until our individualism is set aside and we realize that we are all in this *together*. In other words, "We Shall Be Free," as the four stanzas of the song suggest, when there are no more hungry children, when everyone has a place to call home, when racial discrimination is ended, when pollution of the environment is eliminated, when people are not discriminated against on the basis of whom they love, when people can live with diversity, when religious people quit persecuting people of other religions, when money can no longer buy privilege, and when "there's only one race and that's mankind." The lyrics are as follows:

When the last child cries for a crust of bread
When the last man dies for just words that he said
When there's shelter over the poorest head
Then we shall be free
When the last thing we notice is the color of skin
And the first thing we look for is the beauty within
When the skies and the oceans are clear again
Then we shall be free.
When we're free to love anyone we chose
When this world's big enough for all different views
When we all can worship from our kind of pews
Then we shall be free
And when money talks for the very last time
And nobody walks a step behind

> And there's only one race and that's mankind
> Then we shall be free

The video of "We Shall Be Free" is especially effective. As the lyrics focus on hunger, homelessness, racism, prejudice, pollution, and greed the video depicts not only the effects of these realities, but it also depicts persons and groups of people addressing and combating these realities. A variety of celebrities appear with advice such as "love one another" by ending world hunger and by caring for other people. In other words, freedom will not be unrestricted access to what we individually might want, but rather freedom will be the opportunity to serve one another for the benefit of all people.

At this point, the freedom to which Brooks's song invites us is very close to what the church's mission involves when it follows the pattern set by Jesus Christ. "Love one another," after all, is a quote from Jesus (Jn. 15:12, 17). In short, true freedom is love, as Jesus himself demonstrated in a ministry of justice, compassion, and servanthood. Thus, despite the opening line of the song where Brooks says he's not a prophet, he has managed to be thoroughly prophetic in the biblical sense of what a prophet is—that is, someone who announces God's claim on the world in the form of justice and righteousness that result in *shalom*, "peace." Not surprisingly, the song moves to its conclusion with biblical words like peace, faith, hope, and love. These words allude to 1 Corinthians 13, and the allusion then becomes a quote: "and the greatest of these is love" (1 Cor. 13:13). In short, what humankind, including the church, is called to is love, which is the essence of who God is (see chapter 1).

Taken together, Tracy Chapman's "Why?" and Garth Brooks's "We Shall Be Free" offer complementary motives for the church's mission. As Chapman suggests, the church's mission is a kind of responsibility or accountability that results from an awareness of injustice and our own complicity in it. At the same time, as Brooks suggests, the church's mission is motivated by what "The Confession of 1967" calls "the promise of God's renewal of [human life] in society and of God's victory over all wrong," signs of which the church sees in the "power of the risen Christ."

In essence, the Christian affirmation is not simply that "We Shall Be Free" but that we are *now free,* insofar as we submit our lives and loyalties to God's claim and to God's will for justice, righteousness, and peace. In the words of another confession of faith, "A Declaration of Faith":

> We know our efforts cannot bring in God's kingdom. But hope plunges us into the struggle for victories over evil that are possible now in the world, in the church, and our individual lives.
> Hope gives us courage and energy to contend against all opposition, however invincible it may seem, for the new world and the new humanity that are surely coming.[6]

It's another of the paradoxes we spoke of earlier (see chapter 2). The Christian hope that motivates mission is that "We Shall Be Free," but in a real sense, "The future is now." As we yield our lives to God, as we enter the realm of God, as we follow Jesus Christ in paths of service, as we love one another, we experience *already* the liberating love that is true freedom. To live that love is the church's mission. (Appendix A contains the names and addresses of several organizations that are dedicated to the pursuit of justice, righteousness, and peace; these organizations are ones supported by the artists whose songs are cited in this book, and your support will be appreciated as well.)

NOTES

[1] In the *Book of Confessions*, Part I of *The Constitution of the Presbyterian Church (U. S. A.)* (Louisville, Ky: The Office of the General Assembly, 1994), p. 266 (Section 9.32).

[2] William C. Placher, *Narratives of a Vulnerable God: Christ, Theology, and Scripture* (Louisville, Ky.: WJKP, 1994), pp. 154–55.

[3] Elza Tamez, *The Amnesty of Grace: Justification by Faith from a Latin American Perspective*, trans. Sharon H. Ringe (Nashville: Abingdon, 1993), pp. 134–140.

[4] Mary Pipher, *The Shelter of Each Other: Rebuilding Our Families* (New York: G. P. Putnam's Sons, 1996), p. 94.

[5] Bernice Johnson Reagon, the composer of the song, based it on an article by John Cavanagh, "The Journey of the Blouse: A Global Assembly," published by Winterfest, Institute for Policy Studies. Cavanagh admits that the details of his article are a composite picture. In other words, the message of the song about full-cost pricing is legitimate, even though some of the details are inaccurate.

[6] "A Declaration of Faith," 10, 5 in *The Proposed Book of Confessions of the Presbyterian Church in the U.S.* (Atlanta: Materials Distribution Service, 1976), p. 172.

CONCLUSION

Facing the Music and Changing the World

In conclusion, we turn to three songs that contain the word "change." If there is anything that the earliest followers of Jesus experienced, it was a change in their lives. To repent means "to turn around"; and as we have suggested, those who accepted Jesus' invitation to "repent and believe the good news" (Mk. 1:15) found themselves living in a different world, the world of God's realm, the *real* "real world" where love is the basic reality. To be sure, it seems that a period of adjustment was necessary. The earliest disciples consistently misunderstood what the new world of God's reign was all about (see Mk. 8:31–33; 9:33–37; 10:35–45). But eventually, especially after the death and resurrection of Jesus, the disciples caught on, and their lives and their world were never the same again. Indeed, the transformation is captured well by the song "Change in My Life" from the soundtrack of the movie *Leap of Faith.* The lyrics describe the miserable condition of the singer's life before experiencing God. But after experiencing God, the singer's life is transformed, as the title suggests. The song can thus serve as a reminder that Jesus changed people's lives and still changes people's lives.

No one experienced more radically how Jesus changes lives than the apostle Paul. This persecutor of the early church became its greatest missionary when Christ came along (see Paul's own testimony in Gal. 1:13–24). Not surprisingly, Paul invites others to be changed too:

> I appeal to you therefore, brothers and sisters, by the mercies of God, to present your bodies as a living sacrifice, holy and acceptable to God, which is your spiritual worship. Do not be conformed to this world, but be transformed by the renewing of your minds, so that you may discern what is the will of God—what is good and acceptable and perfect (Rom. 12:1–2).

And people were changed! In fact, the early Christians became known as "These people who have been turning the world upside down" (Acts 17:6).

In other words, not only did Jesus change people's lives, but by changing people's lives, he also changed the world. Eric Clapton's song "Change the World" invites attention to the importance of changing the world. In the movie titled *Phenomenon,* the main character has a brain tumor that gives him extraordinary mental and psychic powers. He uses them to help other people. As the tumor progresses, it eventually threatens the man's life. Clapton's song articulates for the dying man some of the things that he would continue to do if he were able to "Change the World." For us, the song can serve to invite consideration of what we might do to change the world, given our resources and abilities and commitments as people of God.

This consideration is really the culmination of chapter 5 and all the preceding chapters. In fact, Douglas John Hall suggests that the goal of Christian mission is, in essence, to "change the world." According to Hall, because God loves the whole creation, God wills abundant *life* for all people and the whole creation. To be sure, this life is a gift. Thus, in a real sense, "It is not a matter of our making it happen." But, because "God is making it happen...we are called, invited to participate in God's work." To answer the call will mean "to help God 'change the world.'" Hall describes more fully what this will mean:

> And if I am asked, what is life according to your tradition, then I should want to answer not only that it is the hope that points us toward tomorrow, but the courage to believe that what we hope for is in part already realizable today. It is not necessary that two-thirds of humankind should go to bed hungry every night. It is not necessary that children should die before they have had a chance to live. It is not necessary that old people, alone and bitter in their declining years, should be left in hovels in our cities. There is no law that says war will always be. Life is not only looking forward to what could be if only...Life is also daring to think that what we dream for the earth and for our lives in it could become reality. Not because we are such fantastic beings, capable of anything we set our minds to. No, we are rather mediocre creatures in many ways, without much imagination or courage, and altogether too fixed on comfort to be up to much daring where truth is concerned. But God is creating–is daring–a new earth and new heavens. And we are chosen, before we were made we were chosen, to be stewards of God's work in this world. The goal of mission is nothing more or less than this: to participate in our Lord's mission to help creation discover and realize the LIFE that is being offered in the midst of all this death. To help God "change the world."[1]

As we suggested in the final section of chapter 5 when discussing Garth Brooks's "We Shall Be Free," it is hope for the *future* realization of God's purposes that makes the experience of God purposes a *present* reality. Or, as Hall might say, *hope* gives us the *courage* to enact and embody God's purposes here and now–to change the world! Another song by Garth Brooks also offers a helpful perspective on how Christians will view their mission to change the world. The song is titled "The Change." It is a salute to the people of Oklahoma, especially the victims, survivors, and those who provided help following the bombing of the Murrow Federal Building on April 19, 1995. The video features images from the bombing and its aftermath. The song is written from the perspective of someone who helped following the tragedy. It begins with the question of what good has been accomplished by rescuing one more child, given the presence of pervasive hatred and massive evil in the world. The song continues by acknowledging that efforts for change do not eradicate evil and suffering, but the singer suggests that his efforts for change are a sign that he will not let the world change him or his belief "that love and mercy still exist while all the hatreds rage."

"The Change" is a helpful reminder to us Christians that our mission to change the world cannot be measured simply in terms of visible results. As we affirmed in chapter 1, God does not force people to change nor does God enforce God's will. God is love! God lovingly invites the world to experience the abundant life that God offers, and God mercifully forgives us when we fail to respond. When we fail to respond to God's love and God's offer of love, we hurt God and we hurt each other (see chapter 1). When we do respond, we witness to the good news that God loves the world–in Brooks's words, "that love and mercy still exist while all the hatreds rage." To be sure, our witness may not change the world's persistent propensity to reject God's offer of life and the human tendency to pursue life on our own terms. On the other hand, insofar as we witness to and embody the good news of God's love and mercy, we shall experience a change in our lives that in turn will change the world.

For us three authors, as we suggested in the Introduction, the ultimate purpose in inviting people to face the music is to invite them to listen for the gospel, which for thousands of years has been putting people in touch with the God who changes lives, and who changes the world.

NOTES

[1] Douglas John Hall, *Christian Mission: The Stewardship of Life in the Kingdom of Death* (New York: Friendship Press, 1985), p. 98.

How to Face the Music:
A Practical Guide

Facing the Music and How

As suggested in the Introduction, one intention of this book is to provide a means to engage in creative Christian faith development. Such faith development can occur individually or in groups. This guide is divided into two sections. The first section is a song-by-song analysis of the songs discussed in the main body of the book, as they relate to use in group settings. Each song may constitute a separate learning session or may be grouped with other songs by chapter or portions of a chapter. The second section of the guide provides discussion questions and/or activities by chapter.

Here are some practical tips on the effective use of the material in this book in group settings:

1. Necessary equipment:
   a. Stereo with CD player or tape player
   b. VCR
   c. Monitor or TV projector and screen
2. Determine the type of equipment based on the size of the group. A boom box and a small TV may be fine for a small group, but as the size of the group increases, the capability of the equipment needs to increase. Use multiple monitors, large screen or projection TV's for large groups as well as a stereo system capable of engaging the listeners with the sound. The video should be easily seen and the audio easily heard by all participants. This material has a

powerful impact that is greatly enhanced by powerful presentation.

3. Have video tapes cued and CDs marked.

4. Darken room as needed for video to be readily seen.

5. Introduce each song with enough information to
   maximize involvement of the participants.

6. Debrief each song to deepen understanding and aid
   in application.

In terms of legal issues involving the use of recorded
music, you may be guided by the following information from
the Web page of the American Society of Composers, Authors, and Publishers (ASCAP; see www.ascap.com/licens-
ing/licensingfaq.html): "Permission is not required for music played or sung as part of a worship service unless that
service is transmitted beyond where it takes place (for example, a radio or television broadcast). Performance as part
of a face-to-face teaching activity at a non-profit educational
institutions [*sic*] are also exempt."

Part 1: Facing the Music with Eyes Open Wide

Background information on each song is given in the
order that they appear in the main body of the book. Brack-
ets following the artist and song title contain the title of the
CD and/or video collection on which the song can be found.
Some songs are also available as CD singles.

Introduction

Madonna, "Like a Prayer" [Video= *The Immaculate
Collection*]

This is a controversial song and calls for a mature facing
of the issue of racism. Be prepared for strong reaction to the
interracial expressions of affection and the persona of Madonna. The video is a parable; that is, a pithy story from
human experience with one main point. Racism is the focal
point of the video. Call the attention of the participants to
the story line. Madonna witnesses the stabbing of a young
woman by a group of Anglo thugs. An African American
street person is falsely arrested for the crime. Madonna turns

to a church to pray for guidance. Roman Catholic imagery pervades the video: statuary, rosary, stigmata, etc. The burning crosses represent the Ku Klux Klan. Think of the style of the video as a kind of medieval morality play. It is not necessary to view Madonna as a role model to affirm the message in her music. Her CD, from which this song is derived, is dedicated to her mother who "taught [her] how to pray."

Chapter One

Dishwalla, "Counting Blue Cars (Tell Me All Your Thoughts On God)" [CD = *Pet Your Friends*]

Point out to participants the reference to God in the feminine. Be prepared to deal with their reactions. Highlight the poignancy of the song using the material in chapter 1. Ask listeners to consider all their thoughts on God.

Crash Test Dummies, "God Shuffled His Feet" [CD = *God Shuffled His Feet*]

Describe the scene to which the song refers as a picnic that God has prepared. Invite participants to imagine such an event and listen to the questions asked by the people there. Make sure the listeners understand the definition of a parable (see "Like a Prayer" commentary). Prepare them to hear the parable in the song. Alert the group to the reference to bread and wine that could point to the celebration of the Lord's Supper. Ask them to watch for what kind of impression God makes in the song and what they make of that impression.

Tori Amos, "God" [CD = *Under the Pink*]

Set the song in the context of the experience of Tori Amos as the daughter of a Protestant minister. Let participants know that she has a lot of issues with regard to the faith. This song can be seen as her questioning and searching for a valid faith perspective. Be prepared to address the "rough" treatment of God in the song, as well as her feminist point of view.

Joan Osborne, "One of Us" [CD = *Relish*]

This is another controversial song, and the way the participants are prepared can make a great difference in how meaningful the song can be to them. The phrase that bothers some folks is referring to God incarnate as "just a slob like one of us." If the viewers can see this statement as an affirmation of the humanity of the divine Christ, this video can be a faith-building experience. "Slob" equals humanity and all that humanity entails. Direct attention to Michelangelo's painting of God into which the heads of all sorts of people are placed. Mention Joan Osborne's nose ring before the participants do.

Noel Paul Stookey, "For the Love of it All" [CD = *PP&M (& Lifelines)*]

Younger participants may not be familiar with the folk singers Peter, Paul, and Mary. It could be helpful to set their music in historical context. Noel Paul Stookey, who wrote and sings this song (along with Emmylou Harris), is a practicing Christian who sees his music as witness. Point out the breadth of the song in encompassing the whole of Scripture and the Christocentric focus found in the latter portion of the song. Alert the group to the use of "Love" as a synonym for God.

David Wilcox, "Show the Way" [CD = *Big Horizon*]

David Wilcox is a graduate of Warren Wilson College, a Presbyterian institution in Swannanoa, N.C., near Montreat. David brings his faith perspective to his music. Again point out the use of "Love" for God. Set the song in the context of a theatrical production with God as the playwright. This song, as well as "For the Love of it All," is very suitable for use in worship.

Chapter Two

Metallica, "One" [Video = *2 of One (The One Videos)*]

Watching this video can be a powerful emotional experience. Some may view it as quite depressing. However, proper preparation can help move the group beyond a negative reaction to the pain of the situation depicted in the video to an empathetic and compassionate response. Using material in chapter 2, describe the incorporation of the movie *Johnny Got His Gun*, into the video. Showing the Metallica band member discussing the making of the video is a good way to introduce the song. Make certain that everyone understands the nature of Morse Code and knows the international distress signal is S.O.S., or three dots, three dashes, and three dots.

The Smashing Pumpkins, "Bullet with Butterfly Wings" [CD = *Mellon Collie and the Infinite Sadness*]

This song is a cry of pain and brokenness. It is not easy to hear it sonically or emotionally. The temptation for some folks of faith is to avoid such cries. Facing the music means listening to those voices of angst and responding with help and hope. Ask participants to listen for an Old Testament (Job) and a New Testament (Jesus) reference in the song without telling them what the reference will be. In discovering the biblical allusion in this type of song, the group may learn to listen in the new manner described in chapter one.

R.E.M., "Everybody Hurts" [Video = *Parallel*; CD = *Automatic for the People*]

A sermon in itself, the appreciation of this song is enhanced by proper preparation. Discuss the significance of the setting of the video in the isolated gridlock of a traffic jam. Tease the group into watching for biblical references (from the Psalms) and Christian symbols. Ask them to identify with some of the characters in the cars. Hint that the ending will be a surprise and ask them to ponder what the ending might mean.

Natalie Merchant, "Wonder" [Video = *Ophelia*; CD = *Tigerlily*]

Suggest that people look for and recall all the different ages, nationalities, backgrounds, and conditions of the girls and women who appear in the video. Be prepared for the question of why no men appear. See chapter 2.

Billy Joel, "You're Only Human" [Video = *The Video Album, Volume 2*]

The inspiration for this video is the perennial Christmas movie favorite *It's a Wonderful Life*. Billy Joel is the angel on the bridge who leads the young man to see what life would be with and without his presence. Notice the occurrences of the wind in the video and make a connection with the Old Testament concept of *ruach* and the New Testament concept of *pneuma* as the Spirit of God. Use the athletic image of "second wind" to indicate inner resources can be called upon in time of crises.

Collective Soul, "The World I Know" [CD = *Collective Soul*]

This video is a good example of popular song as parable. The point of the parable is that you have to be free of the things of this world to celebrate this world. Walk the participants through the story of the song step by step. Ask them to note what the lead character reads in the paper and to describe his reaction. Note when black and white occurs in the video and when color comes. Watch for the leaving behind of the things of this world as the character makes his ascent up the fire escape. Point out the correlation of the people walking below and the ants on the ledge. Have the "Ants Marching" video by The Dave Matthews Band cued up and ready to play.

Chapter Three

R.E.M., "It's the End of the World as We Know it" [CD = *Eponymous*]

Don't be concerned about knowing the lyrics of this song. No one does except Michael Stipe, and he is not divulging them to anyone. It is rather the feel of the song and the title repetition that is important. Most young people want to move around on this tune so you might consider letting them let loose on it. Adult groups may want to try to analyze the lyrics, usually to their great frustration. Concentrate on the effect of the song and the title's message.

Tracy Chapman, "Heaven's Here on Earth," "New Beginning" [CD = *New Beginning*]

The lyrics are essential to these two songs and may be difficult to understand without some help. Invite participants to think of times they have seen heaven on earth or have had deeply moving experiences similar to those about which Tracy Chapman sings. It is preferable to play these songs back-to-back as on the recording to achieve their fullest impact.

Bruce Cockburn, "Cry of a Tiny Babe" [CD = *Nothing But a Burning Light*]

The style of the song sets a slow, easy mood. Try to prepare your listeners for the slow but deliberate pace of the tune. If they are patient, they will be rewarded with a wonderful retelling of the birth of Christ and the implications of that birth in their lives.

The Dave Matthews Band, "Christmas Song" [CD = *Remember Two Things*]

The connection between the nativity and the passion of Christ is made with great poignancy in this song. There are many shades of meaning possible in the lyrics, and it might be wise to familiarize yourself with them and your understanding of their meaning before you use the song. The reference to Mary Magdalene may be problematic to some who infer a romantic relationship. Alternate renderings of the reference might redirect the discussion in more constructive directions. Nothing should be allowed to detract from the message of the "blood of our children all around" and the call to radical love in a violent world.

Kevin Kinney, "Shindig with the Lord" [CD = *Down Out Law*]

This song is a great way to celebrate Holy Week or any communion service. The mood of the tune is infectious, and it can get the group moving. Try singing along when the words become familiar, especially on the chorus. Repeating the chorus for sing-along emphasis might be helpful to create the context of celebration.

Collin Raye, "What if Jesus Comes Back Like That" [CD = *I Think About You*]

Some songs just preach by themselves. This one by Collin Raye is a good example. It could be set up by briefly outlining the concept of incarnation. It could be used in conjunction with Matthew 25. Or you could let the song speak for itself. A healthy understanding of realized eschatology as the presence of Christ in the here and now will aid the application of this song to the lives of the listeners.

Chapter Four

Todd Rundgren, "Fascist Christ" [Video = *The Desktop Collection*]

This is one of the more challenging pieces of song and sound to be addressed in these pages. One young person described the feel of the video as "a bad acid trip." The analysis was quite accurate. The desire of the artist is to shake you up and take you up in another dimension of sight and sound. Initially the blurred images and mellow music on the screen trace the image of Jesus. Then, abruptly the music becomes manic and the images are hard and cruel. They illustrate the misuse of faith for the sake of profit and repression. Note the singer's words referencing the Bill of Rights and the separation of church and state. The dancing cross becoming a swastika is unnerving, to say the least, yet the oppression of people in the name of Christ is undeniable historically. In the background, the singer is heard to sing about someone taking his God away, as the swirling clouds once more form the face of Jesus and the video fades out. Used wisely, this video can be used well.

Poison, "Something to Believe in" [Video = *Flesh, Blood, and Videotape*]

Young people are great teachers of adults. This song is a prime example of a powerful message delivered by a group most adults dismissed as insignificant. The young people heard the message and made many adults aware of it. Occasioned by the death of his best friend, the lead singer of Poison searches in the song for something substantial enough upon which to build life. Four scenarios are pictured, and each can be discussed at length. Religious hypocrisy, wounded veterans, personal loss, and homelessness make for meaty discussion with most groups.

Sting, "If I Ever Lose My Faith in You" [CD = *Ten Summoner's Tales*; Video = *Sting's Video Hits*]

Differentiating the "holy church" from God may be difficult. Some will hear this song as one of a lack of faith. But if the song is sung to God, then it is the institution that is being rejected, not God. Those in the Reformed tradition should not be too uncomfortable at the iconoclasm of Sting's song in that we, too, have resisted faith in religious institutions and insisted on faith in the God above and beyond them all.

"God Help the Outcasts" [Videotape and CD soundtrack of *The Hunchback of Notre Dame*]

Using the video of Disney's *The Hunchback of Notre Dame*, play the scene in which Esmeralda seeks sanctuary in the cathedral. The juxtaposition of her prayer and the prayers of the "upstanding" citizens conveys the meaning of the song forcefully. If Jesus was an outcast, what does that mean for us when we meet outcasts in our day? Who are the contemporary outcasts who are waiting for recognition as children of God?

Prefab Sprout, "One of the Broken" [CD = *Jordan: The Comeback*]

The song is structured as a monologue from God. Personal in tone, the tune creates an atmosphere where God can be heard speaking in a fresh and challenging way. Encourage participants to relax and let the music take them to the place where they can hear God speak a word that might be surprising. The song is great for mission emphasis or anytime the group needs to get beyond itself to ministry to a broken world. The redirection of piety into social action is a basic prophetic movement.

Blind Melon, "No Rain" [CD = *Blind Melon*]

The lead singer of Blind Melon, Shannon Hoon, died of a drug overdose. This fact heightens the impact of the video. He, like the bumblebee girl, was searching for a place to belong. Ask your participants if they have ever felt like the girl feels on the video. Ask where they have found belonging beyond the gate or where the gate has been locked. "No Rain" falling refers to no tears falling down the cheeks.

Donna Summer, "Forgive Me" [CD = *Cats Without Claws*]

The most effective manner to experience this song is as a guided meditation. Have the participants close their eyes and concentrate on their breathing for a few minutes. Guide them to reflect on relationships with God and with others, giving special attention to where the relationship becomes broken. Play the song while in the meditative state. Debrief the experience at the conclusion of the song, and give people a chance to talk about the healing that they may have experienced. Use as confession of sin in worship.

James Taylor, "Shed a Little Light" [CD = *New Moon Shine*]

Marvelous images abound in this song. From the first lines, attention is focused and the message is riveted into the consciousness. Video editions of this song can be obtained from Taylor's live performance and add to the meaning by showing his expressions and the inclusivity of the players. The song is excellent to use at Martin Luther King Birthday celebrations or any time justice issues are highlighted in the context of community. It could work well in contemporary worship services as well.

Chapter Five

Van Halen, "Right Now" [Video = *Video Hits*]

Make a list of the graphics on the video and go over them either before or after the video. Displaying them during the video could also be an effective means of accentuating their importance. The lyrics of the song are not essential to this application, but the graphics are essential. Each graphic and video image could constitute a separate discussion. Decide how to best use the time and attention of the group. Consider giving the group the choice of which graphics and images to discuss while holding out to them any one they miss that seems particularly appropriate for the group. The song is an excellent tool to teach the concept of intercessory prayer.

The Graces, "Tomorrow" [Cassette tape = *Perfect View*]

Everyone knows someone who needs someone. This song is a strong reminder to care for those whom others forget. The beauty of the tune belies the brutality of the conditions that so many must endure. Create sensitivity to the needs of others using this song and playing it before taking a group to a nursing home or to work with the homeless.

dc Talk, "Colored People" [CD = *Jesus Freak*]

Racism is a difficult but necessary subject to address today. Other songs that have an anti-racist message included in this book are Madonna's "Like a Prayer," Tracy Chapman's "Heaven's Here on Earth," and James Taylor's "Shine a Little Light." As an integrated group, dc Talk not only talk the talk, they walk the walk of racial inclusiveness. Songs like theirs can open up youths and adults to talk about the prejudice that still divides the family of God.

Sweet Honey in the Rock, "Are My Hands Clean?" [CD = *Live at Carnegie Hall*]

An interesting exercise accompanying this song might be to research the origin of the consumer products used by your group. Full-cost price could be determined by such research and the cost posted on the items.

Joni Mitchell, "Sex Kills" [CD = *Turbulent Indigo*]

This is a scary song. It is scary because it is so true. The prophetic cry here is a remedy for complacency. Much discussion can ensue on each issue Joni Mitchell articulates. Take time to delve thoroughly into the depths she presents to the group. Debrief emotional reaction to the song as well as intellectual reaction.

Phil Collins, "Another Day in Paradise" [Video = *But Seriously, The Videos*]

The plight of the homeless is nowhere better depicted than in this video by Phil Collins. He has also put his money where his mouth is and has raised money for the homeless on his concert tours. Use the material in chapter 5 to develop a session on homelessness using this video and additional material available from local social and religious agencies. Note that the song becomes a prayer as the problem of the homeless is seen as a concern for God.

David LaMotte, "Butler Street" [CD = *Hard Earned Smile*]

This song works on many levels. It begins with a reference to the revelation of God in creation and the exploitation of creation in the name of religion. Then the concept of salvation is explored in an encounter with an individual more concerned with winning a convert than connecting in the Spirit of Christ. The last level is the depiction of the Incarnation occurring at a homeless shelter on a city street. Jesus is depicted as one of the homeless who is thankful he is not wealthy, because as such, he would be self-sufficient and not dependent on God. Although the chorus is a peppy tune, the underlying message is quite profound. It is important to stress the satire intended in the song, especially the chorus, which articulates a nonchalant stance toward those in need and advocates a self-serving religious perspective. To purchase CDs or tapes by David LaMotte, call 1-888-495-6575. For information on booking David LaMotte for a performance, call WorkinFolk Agency at 1-800-553-4993. David can be contacted at the following addresses:

Web site: www.davidlamotte.com
E-mail: LowerDryad@aol.com
U. S. Mail: P.O. Box 551, Montreat, NC 28757

Elton John, "The Last Song" [CD = *The One*; Video = *The Last Song*]

Use the video single version, if available. It has an introduction to the song by Elton John in which he makes a plea for help in the battle to prevent and cure AIDS. He gives some important statistics and informs the viewers that a portion of the proceeds from the video will go to organizations working in the AIDS arena. Time needs to be taken with this video, which inevitably evokes a strong emotional reaction not only regarding AIDS, but also regarding fathers and sons and familial dynamics in general. The story of the

Prodigal Son might be recast as the story of the Prodigal Father.

Judy Collins, "Song for Sarejevo" [CD = *Shameless*]

War can seem so impersonal when viewed through a target screen, which appears to be nothing more than a sophisticated video game. This beautiful song personalizes war in a deeply profound manner. It is a quiet, but compelling, telling of the horrors of war from the perspective of a child. Set the stage for the listening of this song carefully. Have the group imagine being in their homes in bed and suddenly hearing bombs dropping. Ask them to think about how it would feel to see fire fall from the sky and destroy your home and your community. Help them see that this is not fiction, but fact for so many people in the world. The song ends with a plea to do something about the tragedy of war. Consider concrete steps to take to get involved with peacemaking.

Tracy Chapman, "Why" [CD = *Tracy Chapman*]

This song raises some excellent questions that provoke theological discussion. Ask the participants to come up with their own list of "Whys." It may be more important to see this song as initiating the process of truth-seeking, rather than concluding the process.

Garth Brooks, "We Shall Be Free" [Video = *The Garth Brooks Video Collection, Volume 2*]

Brooks utilizes the video genre to the fullest extent in this song. In the video collection version of this song, Brooks prefaces the video with comments about his use of the music video. These comments are helpful in understanding not only his videos, but also videos in general. Particularly pertinent is his rationale for the use of real life footage. He contends that no fictionalized depiction of life can be as effective as life itself. Familiarize yourself with the events shown in the video so that you can interpret their significance in context.

Conclusion

"Change in My Life" [CD = Movie soundtrack of *Leap of Faith*]

The infectious gospel sound of this song says it all. Listen and be moved to transformation.

Eric Clapton, "Change the World" [CD = Movie soundtrack of *Phenomenon*]

Use various scenes from the movie *Phenomenon* to illustrate personal and communal transformation.

Garth Brooks, "The Change" [Video = *The Garth Brooks Video Collection, Volume 2*]

Occasioned by the Oklahoma City bombing of the Federal Building in 1995, this video by Oklahoma native Garth Brooks is one of the best examples of the power of the video medium. If participants are not familiar with the events depicted, fill in the details. There are two versions of the song on the video collection available at most music stores. One version shows Brooks in front of screens singing while scenes of the bombing appear. The other version depicts the bombing scenes only. The version with Brooks gives the personal touch of the performer. The version with only bombing scenes focuses on the event and the interpretation of the event in the song. Both have immense emotional impact that a leader needs to be prepared to debrief.

Part 2: Suggestions For Group Discussion

Our hope, as we face the music together, is that we are all changed by the power of God incarnate. One means toward such transformation is thinking together about God, ourselves, and the world (see chapter 1). The following questions, organized by chapter, offer some suggestions for getting people to think and talk together. Remember, these are just suggestions. You, as leader of a group, will know your group, its context, and its experiences better than anyone, and you'll be in a position to adapt and extend these suggestions. Encourage members of your group to be open both to each other and to God's Spirit.

One: Facing the Music about God: Thinking about God

1. When you were younger, what was your thinking (your image) of what God was like? How has that thinking changed?
2. What's the strangest or most bizarre thought you've ever thought about God? Did you tell someone about it? Why or why not?
3. What could you imagine happening if we were *not* encouraged and/or allowed to think or talk about God?
4. Why do you think there are those who are uncomfortable with thinking some things about God, such as that God suffers and is vulnerable?
5. What would it say about God if God *did* suffer and was vulnerable? What would it mean for your faith?

Two: Facing the Music about Ourselves: Valuable and Vulnerable

1. Can you think of a time when you felt something like the wounded man might have felt in the video "One"? What was that like? What did you do?
2. Why are the words of rage and pain in the song "Bullet With Butterfly Wings" (for example, feeling like a caged rodent) so disturbing?
3. Why do you think it is hard to be a human all alone?
4. Why do you get the feeling of a community in the video "Everybody Hurts," even though folks are isolated in their cars?
5. What is your feeling when the music in the video gets stronger and people begin to get out of their cars?
6. Read together Psalm 139:14. How are you a "wonder"?
7. How is the community of faith a "wonder" to the rest of the world (for instance, nonbelievers) in the face of the normal pain and sufferings of life?

Three: Facing the Music about Jesus: The End of the World as We Know It

1. If REM's claim ("It's the end of the world as we know it") is true, how could they go on to affirm that "I feel fine"?
2. How or where have you seen evidence that heaven *could* be here on earth, as Tracy Chapman sings?
3. What are some ways that our response to Christ helps to redefine the world?
4. What are some situations in the world that need to be changed?
5. If Jesus were to come back in such a way as suggested by Collin Raye ("What if Jesus Comes Back Like That"), what would be the *most* surprising way you could think of? Why would that be surprising?

Four: Facing the Music about the Church: All God's Children

1. Why is it disturbing in the video "Fascist Christ" to see the cross transformed into a swastika? What does this say to you about the history of the church?
2. What kind of things does a church do or not do that makes it appear to be broken, as suggested in Poison's "Something to Believe In"?
3. Who are "the broken" (Prefab Sprout's "One of The Broken") in your home, in the church, in your neighborhood, in the world, and what is it we're supposed to be doing?
4. What would it say about the community of faith if we could imagine that Jesus was the first to be dancing around in a bumblebee costume?
5. Why is it important to remember, as James Taylor sings, that we exist together?

Five: Facing the Music about Mission: Sensitivity to All the Sufferings of Humanity

1. In the video "Right Now," what phrase (or picture) caught your attention and why?

2. Why are we often tempted to wait to help others, as The Graces suggest?
3. Which of these justice issues have you put off until tomorrow: racism, hunger, homelessness, greed, HIV/AIDS; war?
4. Garth Brooks sings about freedom in "We Shall Be Free." What are you free *from*? What are you free *for*?
5. What is it that limits our freedom, according to the Brooks video?

Conclusion: Facing the Music and Changing the World

1. If you could change one thing in the world, what would that thing be?
2. How would you do that?
3. Garth Brooks sings of how difficult it is to change something or make a difference in the world. What would be something that would help you deal with the frustrations that come with trying to assist in the building of the real "real world" (the reign of God)?

APPENDIX A

Justice and Peace Organizations

The following is a list of organizations that are devoted to the pursuit of justice, righteousness, and peace. The names of these organizations have been contributed by several of the artists whose songs are cited and quoted in this book. Contact information is provided, in case you would like to add your support to these organizations and their efforts:

By Tori Amos:
R. A. I. N. N. (Rape, Abuse, Incest
National Network)
Telephone number: 1-800-656-HOPE

By Bruce Cockburn:
COCAMO
Co-operation Canada Mozambique
323 Chappell Street
Suite 307
Ottawa, Ontario K1N 7Z2
Canada

Friends of the Earth Canada (Bruce
Cockburn, Honourary Chairperson)
47 Clarence St.
Suite 306
Ottawa, Ontario K1N 9K1
Canada

Mines Action Canada
145 Spruce Street
Suite 208
Ottawa, Ontario K1R 6P1
Canada

Native American Scholarship Fund
c/o Guy Grand
Verde Valley School
3511 Verde Valley School Road
Sidona, Arizona 86330

OXFAM
251 Laurier Avenue, W.
Suite 301
Ottawa, Ontario K1P 5J6
Canada

Unitarian Service Committee
(Bruce Cockburn, Spokesperson)
56 Sparks Street
Unit 705
Ottawa, Ontario K1P 5B1
Canada

By David LaMotte:
Open Door Community
910 Ponce de Leon Ave., N. E.
Atlanta, GA 30306-4212

By Noel Paul Stookey:
The Public Domain Foundation. Established by
royalties from the "Wedding Song," the Public
Domain Foundation (PDF) has been supporting
family and children's service organizations and
grassroots change efforts worldwide since 1971.
Through intensive outreach, PDF identifies and

partners with innovative nonprofit agencies, particularly those engaged in helping families become self-sufficient. PDF also enables other composers and singer/songwriters to establish personally directed, long-term charitable funds, based on the royalties of particularly inspired songs, and to work collaboratively toward social change.

For more information, please contact Elizabeth Stookey Sunde, Executive Director at pdfdn@concentric.net, or visit PDF's Web page at www.pdfoundation.org.

APPENDIX B

Contacting the Authors

Darrell, Cathy, and Clint will be happy to hear from readers of this book who want further information, who have questions, who have ideas to share, etc. They can be contacted as follows:

Darrell Cluck, pastor
Trinity Presbyterian Church
Address: Trinity Presbyterian Church
4501 Rahling Rd.
Little Rock, AR 72223
Phone: (501) 686-5848
Web page: www.trinpresLR.org
E-mail: Cluckiator@aol.com
Home: 501 Napa Valley Dr., #1406
Little Rock, AR 72211

Cathy George, student
Louisville Presbyterian Theological Seminary
Address: 425 S. Hubbards Lane, #236
Louisville, KY 40207
E-mail: CGeorge462@aol.com
Phone: (502) 895-2227

Clint McCann, Evangelical Professor of Biblical Interpretation
Eden Theological Seminary
Address: 475 E. Lockwood Ave.
St. Louis, MO 63119-3192
Phone: (314) 961-3627, ext. 329
E-mail: cmccann@eden.edu
Fax: (314) 961-9063